THE FORGIVENESS EQUATION

John Noble
THE FORGIVENESS EQUATION

MarshallPickering
An Imprint of HarperCollins*Publishers*

First published in Great Britain in 1991 by Marshall Pickering
Marshall Pickering is an imprint of
HarperCollinsReligious
Part of HarperCollinsPublishers
77-85 Fulham Palace Road, London W6 8JB

Copyright © 1991 by John Noble

The Author asserts the
moral right to be identified
as the author of this work.

Printed and bound in Great Britain
by HarperCollins Manufacturing

Scripture quotations are taken from the *New International Version Bible* copyright © 1973, 1978, 1984, by the International Bible Society. Used by permission of Hodder and Stoughton.

CONDITIONS OF SALE

This book is sold subject to the condition that it shall not, by way of trade or otherwise, be lent, re-sold, hired out or otherwise circulated without the publisher's prior consent in any form of binding or cover other than that in which it is published and with a similar condition including this condition being imposed on the subsequent purchaser.

Contents

Acknowledgements	vi
Foreword by Gerald Coates	vii
Introduction	ix
1 The forgiveness equation	1
2 The ultimate disillusionment	5
3 The forgiveness equation – part II	9
4 The unforgivable sin	13
5 Everything but . . .	18
6 It's free – but it'll cost you all you've got!	22
7 You take the first step and . . .	26
8 Facts + faith = feelings!	29
9 Living in the river	34
10 God's hobby	39
11 Go on, I dare you, love yourself!	42
12 Made in his likeness	46
13 Convicted or condemned?	50
14 Grace – the major discipline!	54
15 There's no waste with grace!	58
16 Now grace is yours to give!	62
17 If . . .	65
18 Anoint the stone	69
19 Learning from others	73
20 Forgiving and releasing	76
21 Power to forgive!	81
22 Confession is nine-tenths . . .	85
23 Sorry – you can't blame Grandma	88
24 Grounds for divorce	92
25 Men who heard from heaven	95
26 Have you forgiven God? And what about his church?	99
27 The unacceptable gift	103
28 Priests forever . . .	108
29 Molehills from mountains	112
30 Reprise	116

Acknowledgements

Thanks to friends and family who have lovingly borne with me through the years and helped me to face up to and discover my weaknesses. Particularly Christine, my long-suffering wife, who had every reason to give up on her stubborn, slow-to-learn husband. In fact, by God's grace I am still being changed from one degree of glory to another. The process is slow but steady. Hopefully those who haven't met up with me for a year or two will see a difference. Thanks to Maurice, who taught me so much about grace and forgiveness. Thanks also to Stuart Murray for his extremely helpful comments and suggestions, to my friend Ken Rose, and to my lovely daughter Ruth, whose tireless effort in typing the manuscript enabled us to make the deadline!

Foreword

George Bernard Shaw could have had the church in mind when he observed "The trouble with her, is that she lacks the power of conversation – but not the power of speech"!

Talking without listening is a twentieth-century disease. Practised repeatedly it stifles conversation. So many of us talk without listening to what God may be saying about our verbalised opinions and concerns. All of us have talked without even listening to the often irrational things we say to others (or about others) albeit as a result of our defence mechanisms. Most of us sound braver than we really are.

A few of us even talk as though "nursing and rehearsing" a thing will make our version of events become even more true!

The truth is, our obsession with making a point, fighting to be heard, emphasizing how right we are and drowning out all other perspectives, often detracts from the truth of a situation. It also hurts other people.

Readers of John Noble's quite excellent book have thirty days to discover the truth about God and ourselves. For some it will be a revelation, a first-time experience, and will open us up to new understanding about God and our own make up. For others it will turn our somewhat cold and

The Forgiveness Equation

defensive hearts to a warmth and response to the values of heaven that could be on the earth. His forgiving truth will cleanse, hurts will be healed afresh, and I believe the wisdom contained within these pages will help open a dialogue with God and those around us.

Like many other readers, I also have family members and other friends who at times appear to be uncaring, irresponsible and insensitive. We all go through experiences sensing that we are misunderstood, marginalized and intimidated. Sometimes such experiences, feelings and thoughts make sitting in a room, with someone who had once been a close friend, a painful experience. "The Forgiveness Equation" will change much of that.

How many of us have stood in a room saying to ourselves "I will admit my ten per cent of blame if he (or she) will admit their ninety per cent"? How unlike Jesus who, though he was sinless, took full responsibility for all the dirty, rotten and awful things we have done, or all the good things we could have done but failed to do. He wasn't to blame for anything, and far from being reactive was pro-active, taking divine initiatives to forgive us, cleanse us and bring us back into friendship with him.

Repentance is not what we have to do before God will have us back, as C. S. Lewis once observed – it is more of a description of the route back itself. My prayer is that many readers will find that route and thank God and his servant John Noble for it.

"The first casualty when war comes is truth", said US Senator Hiram Johnson, in 1917. In the war of the nuclear family and in the war of relationships that takes place in the nuclear age – the truth of this book is going to set off a few explosions of love, happiness and reconciliation – all of its own! So here we go.

Gerald Coates, Spring 1991

1
The forgiveness equation

Then he [Jesus] turned toward the woman and said to Simon, "Do you see this woman? I came into your house. You did not give me any water for my feet, but she wet my feet with her tears and wiped them with her hair. You did not give me a kiss, but this woman, from the time I entered, has not stopped kissing my feet. You did not put oil on my head, but she has poured perfume on my feet. Therefore, I tell you, her many sins have been forgiven – for she loved much. But he who has been forgiven little loves little."

Luke 7:44-47

How wonderfully good God is, and how unpredictable. Here am I, preparing to write some lines which, with the Holy Spirit's help might enlighten one or two new Christians or strengthen a few weary, war-torn saints, and – wham! I'm bowled over, knocked out and blessed right up to my eyes, even before I start. "Lord, this is not what I intended. I'm not doing this for myself – I had others in mind." Well, I suppose I'd better let you in on my little revelation.

The Forgiveness Equation

I had just turned to the familiar scripture in Luke 7, recording the harlot's anointing of Jesus' feet, in order to select the verses I wanted to highlight. I knew exactly what I was going to say. It was my intention to underline the principle that Jesus put across to Simon the Pharisee – that he who is forgiven much, loves much. I read carefully through the passage, decided on verses 44-47, and then it hit me like a sledge-hammer. Jesus actually said something quite different! What he actually said was, "her many sins have been forgiven – for she loved much". For a time I was confused. I felt as though the wind had been taken out of my sails. I had always believed that Jesus' act of forgiveness had produced the response of love from the woman, but it was quite the opposite.

I looked up the translations in other versions. I cross-checked the parallel references in the other gospels, only to discover that Luke alone chose to include this part of the story – if, indeed, his was the same story at all. I could find nothing to justify my previous understanding. "A fine start," I thought. "My opening gambit has been completely destroyed." I began to wonder about the rest of my material. Then I pondered over the woman's action and soon found myself deeply moved. At this point Christine, my wife, came into my study and, seeing that something profound was happening to me, asked, "What's the matter, love?" I pointed to the verse in my Bible, opened my mouth and began to weep uncontrollably. It was fully two or three minutes before I could even think about replying. Finally, I choked out my answer through the sobs. Let me try to explain what I had seen as the fresh light had broken into my heart.

This sinful woman – an outcast of society, avoided by all apart from those who only wanted her for her body – saw something in Jesus which, for the first time in her life,

The forgiveness equation

drew from her a totally new kind of love. What she saw caused trust to rise in her heart. She knew that she would never be rejected by him. She had faith in his forgiveness before he uttered a word, and so she risked everything to break through the wall which protected the male domain, in order to worship at his feet. She was driven by love and went with no thought of reward. Jesus was worthy of her praise and honour. She took her most treasured possession and, as if that were not enough, poured her tears along with the precious perfume over Jesus' feet. I had always admired this woman, but suddenly she rocketed in my estimation.

I found myself repenting and worshipping with her before the Lord. So much of my love for him had been retrospective – a response to what he had done, rather than an offering simply for who he was. Her faith humbled me and put me intimately in touch with Jesus once again. I was reminded of Satan's mocking question to God as he went about his business of tempting Job: "Does Job fear God for nothing?" He must have been extremely frustrated as he watched this scene, for here was one who braved arrogant stares and biting whispers and possibly even punishment, to give her all to the Master. However, determined though she was, the glory was not hers.

I asked myself what brought about this extravagant display? What could have motivated the woman even before she heard the words, "Your many sins have been forgiven"? And I realised that once she had caught a glimpse of Jesus, she would not let him go. She had watched his every move – not superficially, but with penetrating gaze – until she had seen *his* glory. She discovered what others missed. She knew he was the One she had been looking for all her life without realising it. Jesus, the light of the world, had won her heart. *His was*

The Forgiveness Equation

the honour, the praise and the glory. Nothing else concerned her. I guess those parting words of Jesus rang in her ears for the rest of her life: "Your faith has saved you; go in peace." Truly, the one who loves much is forgiven much!

Read: Luke 7:36-50.

Pray: Come humbly before God, asking for a fresh vision of Jesus and his glory that will lift your eyes away from yourself and away from your critics. Such a vision will enable you to release your love and adoration to the Lord. He alone is worthy!

2
The ultimate disillusionment

Here is a trustworthy saying that deserves full acceptance: Christ Jesus came into the world to save sinners – of whom I am the worst. But for that very reason I was shown mercy so that in me, the worst of sinners, Christ Jesus might display his unlimited patience as an example for those who would believe on him and receive eternal life.

1 Timothy 1:15-16

I looked up at the crude, black, wrought-ironwork of the huge gates. *Arbeit Macht Frei* – "Work Makes Free" – the words appeared to be etched against the background of the clear, bright, blue sky. I was about to enter the Nazi concentration camp at Auschwitz in Poland, where two million people, mainly Jews, were exterminated in massive underground gas chambers. I cast my mind back to Hadleigh, the small, sleepy Essex town where I had left my wife and five young children whilst I took on the role of Bible smuggler for a few weeks.

Bible smuggling was much talked about amongst Christians during the late sixties and early seventies, when I

The Forgiveness Equation

began making a few trips. Popularised by Brother Andrew, the idea appealed to me for a variety of reasons. We'd be helping the suffering church; we'd learn from their experiences; we'd probably be able to contribute something in the way of teaching and, no doubt, we'd bring back a few tales to chill the spines of the saints back home. But I hadn't bargained for the uncertainties and fears. Were we being watched? Would we get out? And boy, I really missed Christine and the kids. I felt lonely and strangely vulnerable. Well, I certainly got my stories, but they weren't always what I'd expected.

I followed the crowds – mainly schoolchildren on educational trips – into the main site, which had been made into a museum. Although it was a beautiful day, a pall of depression surrounded me. I don't recollect seeing a bird or hearing one sing. As I didn't understand the language, I avoided the guided tour, breaking away to wander around on my own. I looked at models of the shower rooms into which the prisoners were herded after they had been stripped of all their clothes. Their heads were shaved when they were admitted to the camp, and the bodies of many of them became emaciated through weeks of malnutrition and starvation. Finally the prisoners were flung into the gas chambers, and then their corpses were incinerated. The photographs around the walls of the museum told their own stories of fear and incredible suffering.

The primitive wooden huts in which the hundreds of thousands of inmates had lived out their last days stood just as they had more than two decades before. The bunk beds, far too small even for one person, had been occupied by two or three. I could almost hear the crying and groaning as I stood there, trying to take it all in. But there was more. I continued on from room to room, and the horror of what had taken place became engraved on my

The ultimate disillusionment

soul. Here was a heap of artificial limbs taken from the disabled; there was a pile of dentures, clothes, handbags and kiddies' shoes; there was a mountain of teddy bears and dolls.

On and on I walked, until I came to a large barrack room which had been divided into two and partitioned off with glass. All along one side, behind the glass wall, was human hair to a depth of four to six feet. On the other side were bales of cloth stacked on top of one another surrounded by household goods like table-lamps and wallets. I soon learned that the bales were fashioned out of human hair and skin. The latter was taken from the bodies of some of the victims and cured.

I'd finally had enough. Thoroughly sickened, I went to leave, but found myself in a long corridor lined with rows and rows of convict-style photographs. There was a number below each forlorn face. Over some hung limp poppies, revealing the fact that families still mourned the loss of their loved ones long since gone. Then I cried out in anger and confusion to the Lord, "Am I part of the same race of beings as the monsters who committed this horrendous crime against humanity, Father?" And he didn't leave me in silence. The Lord spoke clearly to me, in an almost audible voice: "Yes, son, all these seeds of sin were in you, only the ground was different. What's more, I would have had to suffer and die on the cross in just the same way if you had been alone on earth and these wicked men had never existed!"

It suddenly dawned on me that sin was sin. Had my circumstances been different, then the seeds in my life might have flourished and reached their full potential. Like Paul, I too was the chief of sinners, and nothing less than Jesus' blood could ever atone for my disobedience. I'd known it all along, but now I knew I knew. The relief

The Forgiveness Equation

was indescribable as I saw my sin, and therefore my salvation, in a totally new light. Thankfully, I've never recovered from my visit to Auschwitz, but now I long for others to be completely disillusioned with themselves.

You see, some Christians spend their lives being more and more disappointed with themselves, as they discover areas of weakness or reaction they were unaware of. They are continually saddened and depressed, saying to themselves, "I never realised I was that bad." Furthermore, because they've graded their sin they find it hard to relate to others who appear to be so much worse than they are. God's perspective changes all that and helps us to get things in proportion. We stop dwelling on just how evil we are when we realise we couldn't be any worse!

Read: 1 Timothy 1:12-17; Romans 3:9-26.

Pray: Ask the Lord Jesus to give you an appreciation of the depth of your sin against him and your fellow men. This will increase your love for him and give you an understanding of and sympathy for others. Pray for anyone known to you whose sin is particularly offensive in your estimation.

3
The forgiveness equation – part II

For if you forgive men when they sin against you, your heavenly Father will also forgive you. But if you do not forgive men their sins, your Father will not forgive your sins.
Matthew 6:14-15

We've seen how the one who loves much is forgiven much. Now let's look at the second part of the forgiveness equation: as you forgive, so you will be forgiven. In order to do this I'd like to go back to an experience I had just before I finally came into full-time Christian work back in 1967. Please forgive the expression, "full-time" – it's my firm belief that we should all be "full-timers" for Jesus, whatever our work may be. But I'm sure you'll understand what I mean.

I had started my own business as an advertising consultant with a view to making enough money to support the family. I did this so that I could give myself to a growing preaching ministry which was taking me into coffee-bars, schools, colleges and a multitude of different churches. However, the Lord had very different ideas as to how he would run my finances. The first year was a rip-roaring success, and I built my turnover up to almost £50,000 – which, at that time, in a period of recession, was pretty good. I was feeling quite confident, believing that if I could succeed in this way when things were tough, I would do even better in a boom. But that kind of thinking is purely natural, and I was not ready for what happened next.

Three or four of my best clients went broke leaving me with heavy debts which I had incurred on their behalf. And there was little promise of future work. One of the clients alone owed me over one third of the value of our house, and I decided to take him to court in an attempt to recoup at least some of my money. You can imagine that I did quite a bit of praying. During one of these times when I was seeking God, I found myself repeating the prayer Jesus gave us. When I came to the words, "Forgive us our trespasses", I heard myself using the less familiar word, "debts" – something I had never consciously done before. I continued, "as we forgive those who . . ." and the words stuck in my throat. Try as I might, I could not get them out.

With my mind's eye I could see the faces of those who were in debt to me. I could not escape the fact that the Lord had put me in a corner. I owed money which I could not pay because I was owed money which my debtors could not pay. I needed forgiveness for my debts, but to obtain it I had to be willing to forgive those indebted to me. I kicked and struggled and argued, all to no avail. The Lord did not intend to budge an inch. Had the man who owed me the most had any resources, I think in all conscience I could have pursued him, but he had nothing. The only way forward was to completely set him free.

The forgiveness equation – part II

Eventually I picked up the phone and called him. You can imagine his incredulity and joy – he almost fell off his chair with surprise! It certainly opened the door for me to speak freely about Jesus. I'd love to say that the end of the story was that he was converted, but as far as I know, he was not. What's more, I had to sell my home in order to pay my own debts, and Christine and I, together with our five children, had to live in a condemned house for some months. I moved on into my new ministry without a penny to my name, and I didn't get another house for my family for almost two years – but that's another tale. What I can say is that I wouldn't swap that experience for anything.

Christine, the kids and I learned to trust God in a totally new way. We had no business, church or organisation to support us through those first formative years. The Lord clearly supplied all our needs, often in quite miraculous ways. It was by no means easy, but that lesson has stood us in good stead over the years, and through it we have been able to inspire others to venture down the same path of faith.

The fact that our Father refuses to forgive those who themselves refuse to forgive is not an indication that he is vindictive, although it does show us that he is not sentimental. We must understand that forgiveness is not cheap. The simplest act of disobedience – the taking of one piece of forbidden fruit – opened up the world to a deluge of sin and self-indulgence. Setting men free cost the Father his most treasured possession – Jesus. But it's not even that cost which is of prime importance to God when he refuses to forgive unforgiveness. If he were to allow ungrateful men into the fullness of his kingdom, it would become polluted all over again. Heaven itself would become hell!

The Forgiveness Equation

As a result of all this I came to appreciate God's judgement just as much as his love – indeed, perhaps they are one and the same thing. The fact that he is determined to purge every vestige of sin from us is actually our assurance that our future is perfect. Only those who do not fully realise the cost and the effect of unforgiveness can possibly hold out. Thankfully, the Lord knows our feeble frame and has unlimited patience (1 Timothy 1:16). But this does not mean that those who refuse to seek his face will avoid his anger. For he will surely judge each one of us in the light of our response to his Holy Spirit's prompting.

Read: Matthew 6:5-15 & 18:21-35; 2 Peter 3:8-13

Pray: Open yourself up to comprehend both the cost of our sin to God and the far-reaching effects of our disobedience. Ask the Holy Spirit to bring to mind any from whom you have withheld forgiveness. In order to convey your change of heart you may need to make personal contact with those who have been aware of your difficulty with them.

4
The unforgivable sin

"I tell you, every sin and blasphemy will be forgiven men, but the blasphemy against the Spirit will not be forgiven. Anyone who speaks a word against the Son of Man will be forgiven, but anyone who speaks against the Holy Spirit will not be forgiven, either in this age or in the age to come."

Matthew 12:31-32

"Man overboard!" The cry came from a passenger whose knuckles were white as he gripped the ship's rail with one hand and pointed anxiously with the other to the spot where he'd seen his friend fall into the stormy waters. "There he is. He's surfaced over there. Throw him a lifeline." With speed and accuracy one of the crew grabbed a lifebelt and threw it into the water with a line attached. It landed safely right beside the drowning man, who took hold of it momentarily. Immediately the sailor began to haul in the rope but, to his utter amazement and consternation, the lifebelt was cast aside and rejected. Gathering in the line, he quickly tried again. But this time, in spite of the lifebelt being within easy reach, the man did

The Forgiveness Equation

not even give it a second glance. The sailor repeated the action a second time, desperately shouting, "Take hold of the lifebelt – you'll never survive!" It was too late. There was a gurgle and a splash, and then the man went down. The ripples which he had left on the surface vanished in a split second as their pattern was punished by the wind.

You'll be relieved to know that the episode I've described here never actually happened. It came right out of my imagination. But I believe it will help me to explain what "the unforgivable sin" is. Over the years a number of people have approached me, agonised by the thought that they might have committed the one act of disobedience that would put them completely beyond forgiveness. I have no doubt that many more have secretly nurtured similar fears. Many Christians who are secure in their salvation would have no idea how to answer anyone who came to them with this dread. I therefore consider it important to provide some interpretation of these words spoken by Jesus, which seem so rigid and unbending.

In the case of any scripture, whether easy or difficult to understand, we must examine it against a background of what else the Bible teaches on the same subject. Passages like the one I've referred to should not be taken out of context or viewed in isolation. Jesus gave this warning to religious leaders and hypocrites who were not only opposing him, but were going so far as to attribute his miracles of deliverance, which were wrought in the power of the Holy Spirit, to Beelzebub. This clear and visible evidence of his power over evil spirits and sickness, plus the fact that the good news was preached to the poor, was the only proof of his identity that he would give to the disciples of John the Baptist when they came enquiring, "Are you the one who was to come?"

The unforgivable sin

At no time do the Gospels record that the religious leaders, who plotted against Jesus in order to preserve their status, felt any regret or remorse. They claimed to be leaders of God's chosen people and sons of Abraham, but Jesus told them, "You belong to your father, the devil" (John 8:44). They had no fears of having blasphemed; all their fears concerned the loss of their own reputation and authority. That is why they worked together, and even worked with the secular powers of the day, to rid themselves of Jesus' threat to their leadership and livelihood. I have seen a hint of this kind of arrogant attitude in some of those who have criticised the work of the Holy Spirit in the church today. However, at no time in history have we seen the love and power of God displayed in such purity as it was in our Lord, and so we must be careful not to accuse anyone of the same sin. Nevertheless, there is a serious warning here to those of us who resent and pour scorn upon the obvious spiritual blessings which are manifest in the lives of others. And – please understand me – I do not say this to undermine honest and constructive criticism; this is greatly needed in our Christian relationships today. This is especially true in the case of much of what goes on in the name of the Holy Spirit.

Well, that's the setting. Now, how does our passage harmonise with the rest of the Scripture? One thing is certain: there is no question on the matter of forgiveness of all kinds of sin. Over and over it is confirmed in both the Old and the New Testament that God will forgive those who come with humble and contrite hearts, whatever their sin. Indeed, I trust that my efforts in these pages will positively demonstrate this fact. So, what does the Good Book have to say on the subject of that which cannot be forgiven? There's no space here, nor is it my purpose, to conduct a detailed examination of what the Bible has to say

The Forgiveness Equation

about this. What does become clear as you familiarise yourself with its teaching is that open, intractable and unrelenting rebellion is unpardonable.

Hebrews 6:4-6 shows us that the one who has had a full and complete revelation and experience of God and his kingdom through the Holy Spirit, and then consistently rejects it, has no way back. Scripture here is not referring to normal backsliding, there is indisputable evidence in its chapters that there is restoration for all those who fall and truly repent, even repeatedly. One could debate, as some do, whether any mere human being has had such an in-depth revelation of the future age. That is not for us to judge, but it must be an exceedingly rare experience. Certainly, it would be true of Satan and his angels; there is no hope of a future redemption for them. They stood in the very presence of God and made their choice to rebel from that exalted position, so there is no way back for them. This is where my story about the drowning man may help.

In one sense, all those who become aware of sin in their lives will be able to identify with him. Each one of us needs the lifeline of Christ's saving grace, made available to us through his death on the cross and his victorious resurrection. Now, whilst it was Jesus who died and rose again, it is the Holy Spirit who reveals to us the means of salvation. He opens our eyes to the way of escape. Again and again, in reality, he provides us with the opportunity to respond, just as my fictitious sailor did by throwing the lifeline. We may in ignorance, in panic or through temptation reject Jesus, because we fail to understand what it is that he has done for us. But when we consistently push away the Spirit's clear revelation of the only way into the kingdom of heaven, God has nothing more left to offer.

The unforgivable sin

It is not that our heavenly Father suddenly changes character and becomes moody and vengeful. It is simply that having repeatedly refused the knowledge and proximity of his plan for our salvation, there is no other way for us to find peace with God. God has no Plan B. He gave his best right at the very start, and nothing else could have satisfied his own demands for love and justice anyway. Now, in the light of this, ask yourself the question – do you, with a full understanding granted by the Holy Spirit, continually reject his offer of salvation and forgiveness through Christ Jesus our Lord? Only a fool would do this, and such fools do not feel any sense of guilt or attrition. So, banish the dark thoughts which come from the evil one, open yourself up to the Holy Spirit and look to Jesus, thanking him for his unfailing love towards each one of us.

Read: Matthew 12:22-37; Psalm 51:7-12.

Pray: Thank Jesus for sending the Holy Spirit to enlighten us. Welcome him into your life and worship him for his constant efforts to reveal Jesus to you, in you and through you. Ask his forgiveness for those times when you have offended him and failed to recognise what he is saying. Receive the peace of God, which puts your fears to rest.

5
Everything but . . .

When Judas, who had betrayed him, saw that Jesus was condemned, he was seized with remorse and returned the thirty silver coins to the chief priests and the elders. "I have sinned," he said, "for I have betrayed innocent blood."

Matthew 27:3-4

Thank God that his word does not gloss over the truth, but tells it plainly as it is. This honesty produces confidence and security in those of us who read the Bible prayerfully. We know we can trust what it says. Among other things it contains many sad stories, faithfully recorded for us. Few can be so tragic as that of Judas Iscariot. It was my friend Oliver Nyumbu of YWAM, who when he was preaching for us at one of our summer camps in Scotland, drew my attention to the awful facts surrounding Judas' end. It was a powerful message and led me to ponder the lessons which Judas' story has to teach us.

We have no idea what the thoughts in Judas' mind were which led him to betray Jesus. Was he disillusioned by Jesus' disregard for money and wealth? Was he simply

Everything but . . .

motivated by his own greed? Did he believe Jesus would use his power to escape the betrayal and set himself up as the Messiah? Or had his mind become so sick and twisted that, in some strange way, understanding that Jesus would have to die, he saw himself as the true hero amongst the disciples, the one who would pave the way for that great sacrifice on the cross? We will never know. What we do know is that, whatever the reason was, Satan moved in and took up residence in Judas, directing his every action (Luke 22:3). So it was that he went out to sell his Master for a few pieces of silver and guided the soldiers to Jesus, with a kiss as his signal.

When the full impact of what he had done gripped him, he took several of the steps that the Bible actually calls us to take in the process of repentance. Firstly, he saw clearly the outcome of what he had done when Jesus stood condemned; secondly, he was seized with remorse; thirdly, he returned his ill-gotten gains – the thirty pieces of silver; and fourthly, he confessed his sin before men. You may have thought that this was enough to secure his peace of mind, but it was not. The most important thing was left undone. He did not seek the forgiveness of Jesus. Instead he went out and hanged himself in an effort to ease his torment, but even that was of no avail. There was no way he could avoid the judgement seat and the punishment of God which was his due.

We may argue as to the possibility of Judas' salvation, but the fact is that Jesus did not reject him; quite the opposite. In full knowledge of what he was about to do, Jesus continued in fellowship with him, going so far as to break bread with him at the last supper (Matthew 26:21-28). Furthermore, he acknowledged him as a "friend" right up to the final contact at the very moment of betrayal (Matthew 26:50). Yet never once did Judas make

The Forgiveness Equation

that vital move of throwing himself on the mercy of Jesus the Son, or on that of God the heavenly Father.

Esau, the Bible tells us, was another who could bring about no change in his circumstances, even though he sought it with tears (Hebrews 12:16-17). Being sorry is not sufficient, even when our remorse is accompanied by weeping. Putting things right with others who were a party to, or affected by, our sin will not redeem us either, necessary though that course of action may be. We have to examine our motivation. Why are we upset or ashamed? Are we grieved because we have offended a righteous God or because we've missed out on his blessing or, worse still, simply because we've been found out?

In counselling situations my wife Christine and I often come up against people with these kinds of difficulties. They are so hungry for the joys which they know should be theirs, and sometimes are so full of resentment at what they appear to have lost, that they will do almost anything to obtain those joys, except the one thing that is required. Micah 6:8 tells us precisely what that is – "To act justly, and to love mercy and to walk humbly with your God." We must come to the Lord on his terms, not our own, for our hearts are inclined to deceive us and lead us astray. Perhaps that is why in one of his prayers David asked God to search and test his heart, to see exactly what was hiding away there. When we try to assess our own motives we are likely to fail miserably. Either we will become puffed up with pride and self-righteousness or we will be filled with despair and condemnation, for we have no true measure of judgement apart from the Holy Spirit. His diagnosis may be painful, but with it comes the only medicine which can properly heal our many afflictions – that perfect mixture of grace and truth.

Everything but . . .

Read: Matthew 26:6-30 & 27:1-10; Psalm 139:23-24.

Pray: If you are struggling in this area, confess your inability to repent due to your failure to truly understand what is in your own heart. Seek God's perspective on what is sin and righteousness, so that you can agree with him and take whatever steps he calls for. Most importantly, humble yourself before God and ask for his forgiveness. Here are some simple steps you should take in the process of repentance:

1. Seek God's perspective on what are the real sins in your life. (You may be surprised to discover that some of the things you assumed were wrong are not sin in his eyes, whilst other things you have overlooked completely are of extreme importance to your heavenly Father.)
2. When you see plainly your wrongdoing, confess it clearly to God and to your fellow believers. (See Chapter 22 for more on the subject of confession).
3. Beseech the Lord to help you see how much you have hurt him, and ask for his forgiveness. (Don't wait for feelings of well-being; trust in God's promises to forgive and in his unfailing faithfulness.)
4. With the Holy Spirit's help, turn away from your failure. (With true conviction of sin comes the power to change, although this may be contested by Satan, and a process may be involved.)
5. Where it is possible, make recompense or put right the wrong you have done. (Ask forgiveness of those you have hurt and return money or things you have stolen etc.)

6
It's free – but it'll cost you all you've got!

The kingdom of heaven is like treasure hidden in a field. When a man found it, he hid it again, and then in his joy went and sold all he had and bought that field. Again, the kingdom of heaven is like a merchant looking for fine pearls. When he found one of great value, he went away and sold everything he had and bought it.

Matthew 13:44-46

When I was a child I wasn't very impressed with Sunday School stories. There was always a punch-line tagged on at the end specially designed to get at me in some way or another. No matter how much I was sucked into enjoying the beginning, I learned to retain my scepticism and wait for the moral ending which was supposed to make me into a better boy for mummy. Rarely did these stories uncover the weaknesses of adults, and they seemed to demand a spirituality from us kids which we couldn't always see demonstrated in most of the older folks. Perhaps this was

It's free – but it'll cost you all you've got!

one of the factors that started me off on my quest for reality as I began to grow up.

What's more, I was given to believe that Jesus used simple parables in order that we could understand the truths he taught. Later on, as I began to read the Bible for myself, I discovered that he actually said the opposite. In Luke 8:10 he declared, "I speak in parables, so that, 'though seeing, they may not see; though hearing, they may not understand'." Jesus' stories did not always have a single, immediately obvious meaning. A humble, seeking heart was the key which unlocked their secrets. The parables of the field with its treasure and the pearl of great price are a case in point. "Who is the pearl of great price? What is the hidden treasure?" we were asked, and you didn't need to be intelligent in our Sunday School class to know that the answer to almost every question was "Jesus". "What do we have to give to obtain him?" "Everything!" we cried in unison. It all sounded so right. Who would dare to think that it could be any other way? But somewhere I was left feeling guilty, since, at that time, I wasn't convinced that Jesus was worth such a costly investment. Christians seemed to have to work so hard, and many did not appear to be very happy with their salvation.

Well, I don't wish to deny that this interpretation may possibly have some value. However, years later – and I can't remember who the preacher was – I heard an entirely different perspective which caused my heart to miss a beat. This man of God suggested that I was the treasure hid in the field, that I was the precious pearl; and that it was Jesus who gave up everything to purchase me for himself. At first it seemed too good to be true, but the more I thought about it the more his version seemed to fit the facts. After all, what did I possess that could get

The Forgiveness Equation

anywhere near to buying that which is priceless? And whatever opinion I have about my own value, there is no doubt that Jesus gave his all to redeem me. He must have seen something of great value to him buried deep within me to make such drastic action worth his while.

"For God so loved the world that he gave . . ." of one side of grace, but the other side is that, "for the joy that was set before him Jesus endured the cross". There was no emotional blackmail exerted by the Father upon the Son. He freely chose the path that led to his death and suffering in hell so that he could purchase us for himself. How often have we allowed ourselves to be motivated by the pressure to do what is reasonable, rather than by love? It would be more true to say of some of us that "Because of the duty that was laid on us, we reluctantly did what appeared to be right and never really experienced any return or blessing for our effort." But here Jesus gets all the glory and I get all the blessing – and it's absolutely free. In fact, to even think that we can do anything to obtain our salvation is obnoxious in the extreme.

Okay, to keep the balance I'll not ignore the paradox. It is true that if we're to be disciples of Jesus we must be willing to take up our cross and follow him. So perhaps the first rendering of our two parables has an application after all. But it must be clearly understood that only those who realise that the best they have to offer is but "ash" and "dung" can make the exchange with a glad heart and take no credit for themselves. Our rubbish for that which is more precious than rubies and more desirable than gold – that is the reality, even though sometimes it's hard to let go of the junk which we accumulate in life, and which we are called to lay aside.

Read: Matthew 13:44-46; Romans 5:6-8; Isaiah 55:1-13.

It's free – but it'll cost you all you've got!

Pray: Meditate on what Jesus left behind in order to save us, and think how unsavoury it must be for him to have to watch for feeble efforts to purchase his favour. Ask forgiveness for this, and also seek the Holy Spirit's help to turn irksome duty into a joyful service of appreciation.

7
You take the first step and . . .

Come near to God and he will come near to you.
James 4:8

Let me state it clearly once again – we can do absolutely nothing of spiritual worth on our own. We cannot draw near to the Lord unless he first draws near to us. Having said that, it's also pretty obvious from what Scripture tells us that it is God's desire and very much in his heart to draw all men to himself. For this very reason the Holy Spirit is at work in the earth, seeking to reveal God's love to mankind through Jesus Christ. Right at this moment the Lord is striving to find an entrance into the lives of men and women everywhere, so that he might pour in his light and love. Of course, we are less aware of what is happening in God's heart than we are of what is happening in our own, especially when we are away from him.

Therefore, because God is for us and his hand is reaching out towards us, the *onus* now is *on us* (forgive the pun) to make a move. Actually, it will seem that we took the first step, but in retrospect, and as we begin to know

You take the first step and . . .

more about him, we will discover that the Lord had been at work for years, planning around our lives for just such a moment. As our eyes are opened and we do see what is required of us, then is the time for us to act. It may not be at all easy, but as we step out, even in blind faith, God's arm will be there to strengthen and support us. Let me illustrate this from an incident in Corrie ten Boom's life, told in her book, *The Hiding Place*, published by Hodder and Stoughton.

Together with her sister Betsie, Corrie had been through the most devastating ordeals in the Nazi prison camp at Ravensbruck. In fact, this was only part of a seemingly unending nightmare which she and her family had suffered at the hands of the SS. Betsie's last words before their release were to the effect that they should go everywhere, telling people that no pit is so deep that Jesus has not been deeper. She was confident that their testimony would be accepted, as they had been in a very deep pit themselves. So Corrie faithfully travelled, even in Germany itself, sharing the good news of forgiveness. One day she came to Munich with her message. At the close of the meeting she found herself confronted for the first time by one of their actual jailers. He had been a guard in the shower rooms at Ravensbruck and had been particularly hurtful to Betsie when she was extremely weak and sickly.

As the church was emptying this man approached Corrie. Visions of her sister's pain and suffering flashed before her mind's eye. Then he said, "How grateful I am for your message, Fräulein. To think that he has washed away my sins!" Beaming and bowing, he thrust out his hand. She knew that she had to forgive, but she kept her hand by her side. You can imagine how angry and vengeful she felt, but Jesus had died for that SS man. She prayed for the Lord's help to forgive, but felt nothing. Then she

The Forgiveness Equation

prayed, "I cannot do it, Lord; give me your forgiveness." She stretched out her arm to take his hand, and a current passed through her to him. At the same time there sprang up in her a love which was so strong that it almost overcame her.

In the light of what Jesus has done for us, we dare not withhold forgiveness. When we have seen the extent of his love and the magnitude of his suffering on our behalf, then we *can* take the first step. It may be a cold, calculated act of the will, but if we cry to the Lord he will support us and give us the power to go through with whatever the situation demands. There are thousands of saints throughout history who, along with Corrie and Betsie, can testify to this truth, because they first heard the voice of Jesus saying, "Father, forgive them, for they do not know what they are doing." You certainly may feel as though it's all down to you, but God has been secretly and lovingly at work to bring you to the place where you think you're taking the first step!

Read: Luke 23:26-34.

Pray: As you pray today, expect the Lord to bring to mind those who have in the past hurt you or those you love the most. Think about the fact that your sin nailed Jesus to the cross. Now consciously release them, speaking out words of forgiveness to the Lord. If these folks are aware of your past unforgiving attitude, you may need to share your new perspective and ask them for forgiveness.

8
Facts + faith = feelings!

Though you have not seen him, you love him: and even though you do not see him now, you believe in him and are filled with an inexpressible and glorious joy, for you are receiving the goal of your faith, the salvation of your souls.

1 Peter 1:8-9

It was John Wesley who spoke of "that accursed doctrine of faith without feelings". He was highlighting a particular difficulty which he came across in the lives of many Christians. They were encouraged to "believe" but never had any experience of assurance. It is plain to see from his writings and hymns that he himself was a man who felt his religion deeply. I have no doubt that he was fully aware of that other curse which is common amongst those who seek God – the blight of only believing when you are feeling. These two ghosts, which haunt great numbers of saints, really do need to be banished once and for all. The problem is not only related to our initial experience of salvation, but can also attack us in almost every area of our Christian life, including that of forgiveness.

The Forgiveness Equation

Personally, I believe that the issue is aggravated by living in a society which demands instant answers and a church which has virtually eliminated seeking or waiting upon God. If we don't get what we want, when we want it, in the way we expect it, we think something must be wrong! Here again we Christians face the dilemma of paradox. Should we "seek until we find" or should we believe that "today is the day of salvation"? As we are thinking about matters of life and death, there are no simple answers, since no two sets of circumstances are identical. If this were the case we would not need a book like the Bible, which is full of wisdom, history, poetry, mystery and revelation to guide us. A handbook or manual with an alphabetical index would have been sufficient. Fortunately in the Bible there are principles, basic ingredients necessary to our diet, which we should apply if we are to grow up to be spiritually mature. Facts, faith and feelings are three elements which are vital to our walk with God.

The facts on which our faith is built are there to be discovered and learned. The Holy Spirit reveals them, not just to the minds, but also to the hearts of all those who diligently seek them. Faith is a gift from God, and it enables us to believe the facts of God's grace and mercy as displayed in Christ Jesus and recorded in Scripture. Feelings are the natural result of, and flow out from, God-given faith based on Spirit-revealed facts. But the mistake which so many of us make is to think that feelings are the fuel for worshipping the God who has saved us; on the contrary, facts and faith are that fuel. Neither are feelings the ground on which we forgive others; facts and faith are. King David said in the opening verse of Psalm 34, "I *will* extol the Lord at all times; his praise *will* always be on my lips. My soul *will* boast in the Lord . . . " He did not say,

Facts + faith = feelings!

"I'll bless God when I feel like it." Indeed, in saying what he did, David was declaring that his soul – the seat of his mind, will and emotions – would come under the full control of his spirit. A spirit which, through faith, had been brought into harmony with God's Spirit, and was therefore being empowered to take the steering wheel in his life.

So, because we have received understanding, we may claim faith from God. This enables us to start living in a totally different kind of way, by worshipping God and forgiving others. We do not live in this way in order to obtain blessing, but rather because we have received it in Christ and because he rightly deserves all the praise we can give. Now we can say with David, "I will!" The product of this newfound liberty will be inexpressible and glorious joy as we begin to receive "the goal of our faith, the salvation of our souls". God truly is in the business of redeeming our emotions and giving us back our feelings. He is not an austere Father, remote and insensitive towards us. Quite the opposite – he himself delights over us with great joy and singing (Zephaniah 3:17).

We must never settle for a cold heart, even though it may involve patience and a godly resolve to break through. This determination can only be maintained on the foundation of a knowledge which gives birth to trust. Madam Guyon, a French Catholic laywoman of the seventeenth century, was intent on putting this warm heart back into the spiritually barren religion of her day. As a result she was imprisoned for many years, during which time she experienced a period of total desolation. She clung to what she knew of the Lord whom she loved and continued to worship him one day at a time, since he alone was worthy of her devotion. After some long years of faithfully honouring God in this way, his presence bathed

The Forgiveness Equation

her cell with light and love. Sometimes we forget that we have an enemy who is bent on destroying us, or at least keeping us from a closer walk with Jesus. We need to learn from those who have gone before us that the sweetest victories we will ever enjoy are won in the hardest-fought battles. The lasting result of Madam Guyon's visitation is summed up in this poem, which may well have been written as a result of her experience:

Prisons do not exclude God

Strong are the walls around me,
That hold me all the day;
But they who thus have bound me,
Cannot keep God away;
My very dungeon walls are dear,
Because the God I love is here.

They now, who thus oppress me,
'Tis hard to be alone;
But know not, One can bless me,
Who comes through bars and stone:
He makes my dungeon darkness bright,
And fills my bosom with delight.

Thy love, O God, restores me
From sighs and tears to praise;
And deep my soul adores thee,
Nor thinks of time nor place:
I ask no more, in good or ill
But union with thy holy will.

Facts + faith = feelings!

'Tis that which makes my treasure,
'Tis that which brings my gain;
Converting woe to pleasure,
And reaping joy from pain.
Oh, 'tis enough, whate'er befall,
To know that God is All in All.

Read: 1 Peter 1:3-9; Ephesians 2:4-10; Jeremiah 29:11-13.

Pray: Confess your coldness of heart both in your love and worship of the Lord and in your feelings of forgiveness towards those who have wronged you. Encourage yourself in what you know to be true about Jesus and begin to worship him vocally. Declare your resolve to continue in this attitude of worship and forgiveness, whatever you feel. Thank God that in his time and way, he will give you the feelings of joy and comfort you desire.

9
Living in the river

I will ask the Father, and he will give you another Counsellor to be with you forever – the Spirit of truth. The world cannot accept him, because it neither sees him nor knows him. But you know him, for he lives with you and will be in you. I will not leave you as orphans; I will come to you.

John 14:16-18

One of the great privileges we have in being Christians today is that of witnessing a unique awakening taking place in the church worldwide. Many believe that these streams of renewal, which are touching all denominations and almost every nation, are a preparation and stimulus for a final great ingathering before Christ's return, and that they will flow into one mighty river. Certainly the Lord is purifying his church and making her ready as a bride for her husband. In my opinion, the two major signs that the last days are upon us are the outpouring of the Holy Spirit upon all flesh (Acts 2:17) and the preaching of the good news to all peoples (Matthew 24:14). Both of these things are beginning to take place, and where they

Living in the river

are happening churches are growing in quality and in numbers. In the light of this and all that Scripture teaches it would be positively wrong to pass over the importance of the Holy Spirit's role in melting our hard hearts and empowering us to forgive and minister the gospel to others.

Jesus promised that although he would not be with us physically after his ascension, he would send us another Comforter like himself, not only to be with us but to indwell our very beings. From earliest times Christians have testified to an experience which assured them that the Spirit had come and taken up residence in their lives; an experience which enabled them to live every day in the flow of his life. Whilst they may have disagreed about the theology of what had happened, there is no doubt that it was the coming of the Holy Spirit which made all the difference. For example, Wesley tells of his "heart-warming" experience which took place on 24th May 1738 at a meeting in Aldersgate Street, London. Samuel Brengle, one of Booth's Salvation Army leaders, was smitten by God at 9:00 in the morning on 9th January 1885, whilst walking across Boston Common during his devotions. Brengle said, "He gave me such a blessing as I never had dreamed a man could have this side of heaven." Today there are almost 400 million charismatic and pentecostal Christians who have similar stories to tell, and they are part of the fastest-growing movement in the church's history.

This is not the place to tackle the vast subject of the work of the Holy Spirit – and anyway, plenty of excellent books on this subject have been written. Indeed, my wife Christine and I have written *Everyman's Guide to the Holy Spirit – the End of the World and You*, which is published by Kingsway. It covers much of the ground in a simple

The Forgiveness Equation

and readable way and offers practical help to those seeking the fulness or baptism of the Holy Spirit. So I would encourage you to read, learn and pray about receiving and maintaining the Holy Spirit's presence in your life. There are many sides to his personality. I've already spoken of him as the Spirit of revelation, but he is also your Counsellor, your Comforter and the One who empowers you to live. Without him as your constant companion it is impossible to practise forgiveness and to properly sustain relationships. He is your source of strength and will never, ever leave you. My own life would be like a waterless desert without the Holy Spirit. Let me share just two experiences which deeply affected me and brought me closer to Jesus. These stories also serve to illustrate the fact that the Spirit is not limited by our surroundings, by places or by our circumstances, if our hearts are towards him.

I had come from a Salvation Army background, so when I came back to the Lord soon after I was married, I quite naturally returned to my SA roots for fellowship. The nearest corps was in a tiny building which was heated in the winter by an old coke fire, the fumes of which made us all choke our way through the meetings. The music was supplied by a small, out-of-tune pedal organ which squeaked and wheezed as it was played by an elderly lady, who did the same! The regulars who attended consisted of about half-a-dozen folks, two of whom were quite deaf and frequently sang totally different hymns to those announced. One of these was the Sergeant-major, who shouted "Hallelujah!" in all the wrong places. The lady officer was a gem and faithfully served us in preaching and giving opportunity for us to come to the "mercy seat" to get right with the Lord. Who would have thought that in

Living in the river

such a place God would have met with a young advertising executive like me? But he did, time and time again.

I well remember one Sunday morning when the Holy Spirit convicted me of my wrong attitude towards my wife and children. At the close of the meeting, when the altar call was given, I went forward and fell on my knees at the penitent form. The Captain came and knelt beside me to pray, and there I cracked under the revelation of just how hurtful I had really been. All my arguments and self-justification rolled away, and I went home, walking on air, to seek forgiveness from Christine and the kids. I do believe that this experience was the beginning of a process that saved my marriage, which had been very shaky up to that moment.

The second episode occurred in an Anglican church. It was Easter time and we were staying with my family over the break. I can't recall why we chose to go to this particular church, as it was rather formal and packed to the doors with a mainly elderly, middle-class congregation. Both vicar and church were dressed immaculately, he with his fine robes and the church with its glorious spring flowers. Even the congregation were togged out in their Easter best. Nothing was out of place. The familiar words of the Holy Communion were repeated with precision and accuracy. Everyone knew exactly what to expect. Here again the Holy Spirit began to move within me. This time he was showing me just how much it cost the Lord Jesus to suffer and die on the cross for me. I wanted to cry, but felt these people would not have understood, so I held back the tears. But crying and laughing are very similar in that the more you try not to, the more you feel you must. Finally, I could no longer contain my grief and it burst forth in uncontrollable sobbing.

The Forgiveness Equation

Apart from a fraction of a second's hesitation, the proceedings were completely unaffected and continued faultlessly to their conclusion. The people filed out and went their homeward way. No one questioned me or spoke to me. It was as if nothing unusual had happened. But I was never quite the same again, as the Holy Spirit had given me a fresh vision of Jesus and his tremendous love for humanity. That morning the words of "When I Survey the Wondrous Cross" took on deeper significance and my heart was locked even more firmly in the grip of Jesus' grace. The value of these kinds of moments cannot be overstated. They will differ for all of us, but are nevertheless vitally important if we are to continue in harmony and forgiveness with our families and our brothers and sisters in Christ. Only the Holy Spirit can keep us soft and pliable in this way. Let us welcome him daily into our hearts, our homes and our congregations, so that we stay in the centre-stream of the river of his love.

Read: John 14:15-27 & 16:7-15.

Pray: Humble yourself before the Lord. Put aside your reserve and kneel or even prostrate yourself, acknowledging your need of the Holy Spirit. Ask the Lord to fill you, to baptise you afresh with his love. Worship him in the Spirit; even your groans and sighs will mean something to him. Abandon yourself and be ready to speak in a new tongue, should the Holy Spirit give you that ability.

10
God's hobby

Jesus said to them, "It is not the healthy who need a doctor, but the sick. I have not come to call the righteous, but sinners."
Mark 2:17

Why is it that the weak are constantly tricked into believing that they must become righteous before they can approach the Lord, while the strong feel they don't need him? In this way Satan can keep us all from God's love and blessings. There is no possibility of us improving ourselves in order to come to him. Our condition is the very reason we need him. So why should we waste our time trying to change ourselves first? As for those who have got their act together and are secure in themselves, they are in a very dangerous position, for there are "none so blind as those who won't see". Jesus stated plainly that it is "hard for a rich man to enter the kingdom of God!" (Luke 18:24).

My friend Maurice decided that he wanted to be a real man of God. He determined to fast and pray for six days in order to see God's power released into his life and ministry. As soon as he started seeking the Lord he became ill with

The Forgiveness Equation

kidney stones which caused him colossal pain. He became bitter and angry and took to his bed. "Why, Lord, when I seek you in this way, should this happen?" he cried in his anguish. "I only wanted to serve you, but now I can't take any more of this pain. I'm finished. I know you love me, but I've had it. I'm opting out. I'm a failure!" For the first time in thirteen years as a Christian he swore, and he even tore at his pyjamas in his frustration.

Buttons flew in all directions, and he slumped back on to his pillow, firmly convinced that his rejection of the Lord was the end of his walk with God. He lay there waiting for the cloud of depression to descend, but it never came. Instead he felt an incredible sense of peace all around him in the room. "Lord, this is not what's supposed to happen. Didn't you hear me? I'm opting out! I'm a failure!" he repeated, as if God were deaf. Then he heard the Lord speak as if he were in the room with him: "Son, didn't you know? I collect failures! At last you've qualified."

Jesus delights to help those who know they cannot help themselves. In those circumstances he gets all the glory. On the strength of this story another friend of mine announced in a meeting, "John Noble's hobby is collecting postage stamps, but God's hobby is collecting failures. He used to collect stars, but some time ago he completed his collection. Now he concentrates on failures and he has plenty of room for more." Facing up to the reality that none of us is good is a wonderful release to all but the irreversibly proud. It means that we become children of God's grace. And the more we depend on his goodness, the more we are able to understand and relate to others who know that without Jesus they are failures too.

There is no shame in discovering this, even though the world may try to convince us that we shouldn't need any sort of support. They try to tell us what we already know – that

God's hobby

Christianity is a kind of crutch for the feeble and weak-minded. In fact they've missed the point altogether. Jesus hasn't done a patch-up job; he's given us an exchange – new life for old. In him you are an altogether new creation, as old things have passed away and everything is new (2 Corinthians 5:17)! The Lord says to us, as he did to Paul, "My grace is sufficient for you, for my power is made perfect in weakness" (2 Corinthians 12:9). So, in the words of that powerful chorus, "Let the weak say, 'I am strong,' and let the poor say, 'I am rich,' because of what the Lord has done for us." And in the words of Jesus, "Blessed are the poor in Spirit, for theirs is the kingdom of heaven" (Matthew 5:3).

Read: Mark 2:13-17; Luke 18:18-27; 2 Corinthians 12:7-10.

Pray: Come to the Lord Jesus just as you are. Stop all your attempts to overcome your weaknesses or to explain them away before you approach him. He knows everything there is to know about you and is waiting to receive you. Perhaps you would like to worship Jesus by singing or simply saying these words:

> *Jesus, take me as I am,*
> *I can come no other way;*
> *Take me deeper into you,*
> *Make my flesh life melt away.*
> *Make me like a precious stone,*
> *Crystal clear and finely honed;*
> *Life of Jesus shining through,*
> *Giving glory back to you.*

Dave Bryant, © Thankyou Music 1978

11
Go on, I dare you, love yourself!

Jesus replied: " 'Love the Lord your God with all your heart and with all your soul and with all your mind.' This is the first and greatest commandment. And the second is like it: 'Love your neighbour as yourself.' All the Law and the Prophets hang on these two commandments."

Matthew 22:37-40

In the same way that John, in his first letter, shows us that there is an inextricable link between our love for God and the love we show to our brothers, so Jesus reveals that there is a similar tie between the love we have for ourselves and the love we are to show to our neighbour. I would go so far as to say that you cannot love yourself, any more than you can love God unless you have first experienced and received his love for you (1 John 4:19). When you think about it, it's fairly logical to believe that if you have a false appreciation of your own value, then your understanding of the worth of others will be warped. If you think of yourself too highly, you will tend to undervalue others. If you have a low opinion of yourself, you are likely to overrate the gifts and abilities of others.

Go on, I dare you, love yourself!

I was counselling a young Christian man at Spring Harvest one year. It was late at night and I was tired after a full day's ministry. I sat and listened to his story. First he told me the headlines – "I have a cancerous foot, I suffer from asthma and I have a low self-opinion," he said for starters. Then he began to tell me a little about his background. When he was a five-year-old his father had stood him on a high wall, held out his arms and shouted to him, "Jump". The little lad in his innocence obeyed, and as he launched himself into the air his daddy stepped to one side, allowing him to fall on the gravel, where he badly grazed his elbows and knees. As he struggled to get up his father said, "Let that be a lesson to you. Never trust anyone in this life!"

As I listened I found two emotions at war within me – sentiment and anger. On the one hand I felt sorry for this young man, and on the other hand I felt angry that as a Christian he could calmly state that he had a low self-opinion. I could understand all the reasons for his continuing problem, but no-one had been able to help him, and I guessed he'd had a few good doses of sentiment. Everything within me wanted sentiment to win and, furthermore, I was tired. I tried to convince myself that I should just pray for his ailments and go to bed, but finally anger prevailed. "You say you're a Christian?" I enquired in a firm voice. His reply was positive: "Yes, for quite some time," he answered. "Well," I said, "if you call yourself a Christian, it is time to repent of your sin and ask God's forgiveness. Your attitude is tantamount to blasphemy."

His eyes opened wide and would have turned in different directions of they could. I think he was just about to call out and ask if he could have a change of counsellor, but I beat him to it. "My friend," I continued, "when the Lord made you he took a great deal of time and trouble.

The Forgiveness Equation

He put a lot of thought into creating you. You're not the product of chance, a random selection of particles. You are his treasured creation. What's more, you are made in his image and you are unique. There's no-one else quite like you and you are precious in his sight. Your heavenly Father is proud of you!" I waited; his face was expressionless. Had I blown it? Would he punch me on the nose and rush out into the night?

After what seemed an interminable pause he spoke in a stunned voice: "I'd never thought of it quite like that. I suppose you're right." I breathed a sigh of relief inwardly, whilst maintaining my firm look. Then I suggested we pray together. We put things right with God and brought all the past damage and hurts which his father had inflicted upon him to the Lord and asked for healing. Together we pleaded for forgiveness for attributing to our heavenly Father the weaknesses we saw in our earthly parents. Then I asked him to thank the Lord for the way that he was made as a unique son of the living God. Once we had been through this procedure I felt free to pray for his physical needs – for his foot and his asthma. I'd love to be able to tell you that both were completely cured, but I never did hear the end of the story. All I can say is that when the young man left the counselling room he was a great deal happier than he had been when he had come in.

To think wrongly about yourself is almost as bad as having a twisted image of God. In fact, they are usually linked together. When we know the Lord well, we know that he thinks we're the bee's knees! We learn the difference between genuine limitations and inflicted wounds and are able to accept ourselves in truth. Coming to terms with ourselves and learning to love ourselves with the love of God gives us security and power to love our neighbour in the same way. We don't need a magnifying glass to

Go on, I dare you, love yourself!

exaggerate our gifts; nor should we reverse it and in false humility minimise who we are. We are who he has made us. Go on, I dare you, love yourself!

Read: Matthew 22:34-40; 1 John 4:13-21; Psalm 139:1-18.

Pray: Call upon the Holy Spirit to help you see if you have a wrong concept of your heavenly Father and thus a jaundiced view of who you are. Thank him that you were made in the image of God and that you are unique. Commit your uniqueness to his service and seek for his love to flow through you so that you can love others.

12
Made in his likeness

Then God said, "Let us make a man in our image, in our likeness, and let them rule" . . . – male and female he created them.

Genesis 1:26-27

Continuing the theme of our likeness to God, there are some mind-blowing facts that we need to appreciate. I've pointed out that each one of us is truly an individual – unique and created to reflect something of God's nature and character. But beyond this it is vital that we realise that we have also been created for fellowship, not primarily for service or obedience. Secondly, we were not made to be alone, and only together can we adequately display the image of God in all his diversity. Thirdly, we were fashioned to rule, alongside our maker, over the universe and over all other created beings, including the angels. Let's think about our fellowship with God first.

The very thing that Adam and Eve grasped for in disobedience – to be like God – was the thing he wanted to give them freely through obedience. His desire was that, by submitting themselves to his word, they would take authority in the garden, discover the tree of life and in eating of its fruit, live forever in full-blooded fellowship with him as mature sons and daughters of God. In his kindness, when they fell, God banished them from paradise, lest they should find the tree of life and live eternally in their sinful state. Then began the slow and painful process of redemption. The depth of God's commitment to us is shown by the fact that he sent his only Son to die in our stead. Always, as with any good earthly father dealing with a wayward child, the Lord's goal was restored fellowship, never a permanent authority structure. God's authority, whilst it is eternal and absolute, is only ever used as a means to an end; it is not the end itself. Love, friendship and fellowship are his goals. He takes no delight in restricting his children and keeping them by force under his law. Rather, he longs for a complete and unshackled relationship of love.

Our heavenly Father's objective, which he is sure to achieve, is to bring us into his presence, where he can shower us with his loving kindness and give us all things in Christ to enjoy richly forever (Ephesians 2:6-7 and 1 Timothy 6:17). For this reason, through trusting in his atoning death on the cross and in his resurrection from death and hell, we become joint heirs with Jesus. Whilst our God never loses control, he certainly has no authority complex; he has determined to share all he has with us. However, no one man or woman can contain all of his glory. We are, therefore, called to be one people or nation together under God, and as such we will provide a proper channel for the full, visible manifestation of all his wisdom and power.

In his creation our heavenly Father is infinitely diverse, but in his diversity there is always harmony. Unity without conformity means that each one of us maintains his or her identity and also has a special part to play. This is most

The Forgiveness Equation

beautifully expressed in the relationship between male and female. There is no conflict here. We were made to be together; alone, we are incomplete. In the earthly and physical terms of marriage we mirror the ultimate and higher union of Christ and his church (Ephesians 5:31-32). But even more than this, we must also see an expression of the breadth of God's all-encompassing love, which can only be observed when men and women from every tribe and tongue and from all social strata flow together in love, worship and service. So a strong, corporate identity which does not deny our individuality is something which God has ordered and which we should, therefore, cherish if we are to rule and reign with him together.

This means that we must be willing not only to "preserve the unity of the Spirit" but also to seek to "attain to the unity of the faith" (Ephesians 4:3 & 13). The unity of Spirit was given to us at our conversion, and we are called to maintain it. What's more, the visible unity of the faith is not a remote option for us Christians; it is at the centre of God's purpose for us. It was the thing that Jesus prayed for in order that the world might see and believe. All the time we foster or even tolerate divisions, we are giving our assent to the delay of the Lord's return. We are, in effect, saying, "Even so, do not come quickly, Lord Jesus." Of course, the way forward is not through compromise, but through honest and loving dialogue, affirmation and friendship. We are obliged by Christ to walk this path, seeking supportive relationships wherever we see Jesus honoured. We must repent of all divisions which occur in the body of Christ, be they divisions of sex, race, class or doctrine. We must seek forgiveness, first, for the pain we have caused Christ himself by tearing his body apart, and secondly, for the wounds we have inflicted on one another. When we do this we will more

Made in his likeness

perfectly represent God and his kingdom in the dark world in which we live.

As we accept the fact that we were all made in God's image and are reconciled to the Lord and one another, so we more perfectly represent him here on earth. This love and practical unity of faith becomes the foundation for us to begin to take up authority and work together to subdue the earth. As Christ's visible body we can demonstrate his power over the devil, disease and death by becoming a channel through which his future kingdom is displayed in the here and now! The Father's love and justice, which were first clearly manifested in the Son, can now be seen in the Son's bride. Only together can the church effectively commence her reign alongside Jesus in his throne, from whence we are destined to rule with him over all things.

Read: Genesis 1:26-28; Ephesians 4:1-16; John 17:20-26.

Pray: Ask the Lord to give you an appreciation of his concern for the visible unity of his church throughout the earth. Thank God for your own sex and for your own people and their distinctives, and pray for a genuine love, respect and openness for all others who truly love Jesus. Ask him to show you where you have contributed to the divisions in his church, and where necessary take action to give and receive forgiveness.

13
Convicted or condemned?

The law of the Lord is perfect, reviving the soul. The statutes of the Lord are trustworthy, making wise the simple. The precepts of the Lord are right, giving joy to the heart. The commands of the Lord are radiant, giving light to the eyes. The fear of the Lord is pure, enduring forever. The ordinances of the Lord are sure and altogether righteous. They are more precious than gold, than much pure gold; they are sweeter than honey, than honey from the comb. By them is your servant warned; in keeping them there is great reward.

Psalm 19:7-11

Conviction or condemnation – what's your experience? There is a difference, and it's imperative that we know what the difference is. One is from God and brings with it the solution to our dilemma of sin; the other is from the devil and constantly increases the burden of guilt we carry until we are crushed. Which is which? How can we recognise the difference? Are we channels through which God's truth or Satan's lies are communicated? In other words, are we part of the problem or part of the answer? I

Convicted or condemned?

ask these questions not only for our own benefit but out of concern for others as well. For, whether we like it or not, we pass on to the people in our orbit our joys and sorrows, and our blessings and curses.

Haven't you noticed how that when a Christian reads a book which really convicts him or her, the first thing he or she does is to lend it to someone else? I'm sure that's why Arthur Wallis' book on fasting is so popular! Joy and guilt can be equally infectious, and like a highly contagious disease, either can spread with tremendous speed through a family, fellowship or community. Strangely enough, both can feed off lies or truth for their sustenance. Joy based on lies is as deceptive as guilt based on truth. The only difference is that you're happier in the first instance, but nonetheless deceived. Let me give you an example of guilt based on truth.

For most of us it is true that our prayer life is not all that it should be. We could do with more prayer. My friend Gerald Coates was speaking at a church meeting on grace. He was explaining that we do not pray or read our Bibles because we have to and that God's love for us is not based on our performance. Suddenly a man sprang to his feet and interrupted the message. "The trouble with young people today is that they don't pray enough! Our youngsters should spend more time on their knees!" he bellowed in a sanctimonious voice. Gerald is seldom lost for words, but he wasn't at all clear how to deal with this situation. He sent a quick prayer in the direction of heaven. "Yes, our young people should pray more," the man went on, warming to his theme with a religious fervour. At which juncture his wife, who up to this time had been quietly seated next to him, intervened. Thrusting her finger under his nose, she confronted him in a way which led one to believe it was not the first occasion she had done it:

The Forgiveness Equation

"Why don't *YOU* pray more yourself, then?" she screamed at the top of her voice. Gerald's prayer was answered. He had nothing else to do but continue with his sermon. The couple had illustrated his point perfectly.

The man had spoken the truth but he had ministered condemnation out of his own guilt, and that will never produce life. On the matter of prayer, Jesus was so effective in receiving answers that his disciples came to him pleading, "Lord, teach us to pray." What a difference! Jesus prayed out of a conviction which brought results and encouraged others into a life of prayer. It is conviction which comes from God, and when he brings conviction he supplies the resources or strength to enable us to respond. When Jesus said to the woman taken in adultery, "Go now and leave your life of sin", it was not said with frowns and threats, but with love for her and confidence in her, and he made it quite clear that he in no way condemned her.

On the other hand, condemnation mixed with just enough truth is the devil's concoction to poison God's people and keep them at work on the treadmills of guilt, failure and self-justification. With it he can effectively stop our celebrations and our spiritual welfare alike. He can empty churches and bring people into bondage to religious bigots. He can ruin our testimony and destroy our simple love for Jesus in no time at all. Condemnation not only breeds spiritual sickness but can affect our physical health too. It is like a poisonous gas which has very little smell, but we must learn to recognise the symptoms it produces so that we can apply the antidote – true conviction from God's Holy Spirit himself.

Conviction may be painful; we may shed many tears when it is applied to our lives. But always, hard on the heels of God's gift of conviction, follows his gift of repen-

Convicted or condemned?

tance, and not far behind this is the joy of forgiveness. The joy of the Lord is our strength, and we must never forget that, for joy and condemnation can have no fellowship. When I saw just how evil and pressurising condemnation was, I found it incredibly difficult to forgive those who ministered it, and I still do. For religious hypocrites use it to keep people chained to systems and to their power. But the amazing thing is that, although Jesus hated their sin, he loved even the hypocrites and wept for them too. What a Saviour we have. In him there is forgiveness for all who cast themselves on his mercy.

Read: Romans 8:1-4; John 8:1-11.

Pray: Sensitivity to discern the subtle differences between the convicting power of the Holy Spirit and the condemnation of the accuser is essential for every believer. Condemnation produces guilt, while the fruit of conviction is repentance. If you are living under condemnation, pray for divine strength to break free, and then ask the Lord to give you the ability to help lift the blanket of condemnation in the lives of others. Pray too for wisdom and courage to deal with religious bigotry and those who use the pressure of emotional blackmail.

> *No condemnation now I dread,*
> *Jesus, and all in him is mine;*
> *Alive in him, my living head,*
> *And clothed in righteousness divine;*
> *Bold I approach the eternal throne,*
> *And claim the crown, through Christ my own.*

Charles Wesley

14
Grace – the major discipline!

See to it that no one misses the grace of God and that no bitter root grows up to cause trouble and defile many.
                                                    Hebrews 12:15

Grace is not a medicine which, if a small dose is taken, will once and for all cure every ill. Rather, it is a river or an ocean of life-giving water in which we must live every moment of every day. Every single letter which the great apostle Paul ever wrote began and ended with "grace". And it is clear from his writings in general that this use of the word "grace" was not merely a formal religious introduction and benediction. He knew what grace meant in his own experience. According to Romans 5:17 it was "God's abundant provision of grace" and the resulting "gift of righteousness" that enabled Paul to "reign in life".

My friend Maurice, whom I referred to in an earlier section, was unimpressed by the usual Christian definition of grace – "the free, unmerited favour of God". It was true, but somehow it didn't do much for him. So he picked

Grace – the major discipline!

warps our minds and can even affect our physical well-being. If it remains undealt with it smoulders on, and many are hurt or corrupted by the effects in our lives.

With the Spirit's help we must reject the temptation to indulge ourselves in selfish introspection. We are called to keep short accounts with the Lord and with one another when it comes to sin. However hurt or hard-done-by we may feel, we must cry out to Jesus for his help and forgiveness, and then we must forgive and be forgiven. This really is the only way to live, every moment of the day drawing upon the never-failing grace of the Lord Jesus Christ. This is the one discipline above all others which we can never afford to neglect. Just keep on bathing in the river of the Lord's incredible grace. The result will be the constant enjoyment of his forgiveness and a pure stream of love flowing out from us to refresh those around.

Read: Matthew 27:32-44; Psalm 86:1-13.

Pray: Keep short accounts in your relationship with the Lord and with your family and friends. Seek his help to make the receiving of grace a habit in your life. If you tend to hold on to a grudge or indulge in self-pity, you need to cry out for a special anointing from the Spirit to break the grip of that power. Thank him that his grace never runs out and that it is readily available to all who ask in repentance.

15
There's no waste with grace!

And we know that in all things God works for the good of those who love him, who have been called according to his purpose.
Romans 8:28

Grace is the great message of the Bible, yet few of us have understood the extent of God's grace manifested in Jesus Christ. It is infinite in its availability and in its power. Grace not only delivers us from the past effects of our sin, but also releases us from its present grip and gives us faith for the future. Grace is so strong and effective that it reaches out to us whilst we are in sin. Then, when we give our sin to God, he even uses it for his glory and our blessing. The apostle Paul emphasized grace to such a degree that his hearers were almost convinced that it would be of benefit to sin in order to receive more grace. Listen to some of his arguments.

In Romans 5:20 he declares that "where sin increased, grace increased all the more"; in verse 14 of chapter 6 he says, "you are not under law, but under grace"; and then back in verse 1 of the same chapter he asks the million

There's no waste with grace!

dollar question, which had obviously sprung into the minds of some: "Shall we go on sinning that grace may increase?" Perhaps some immature saints had begun to believe that they could even do the Lord a service by continuing in their wickedness so that he would have more opportunities to display his love for sinners. Paul's reply, according to the New International Bible, is "By no means!" But I like J. B. Phillips' rendering much better, even though it is somewhat dated; he translates it as "what a ghastly thought!"

Nevertheless, the fact remains that when we do sin and truly repent, God actually uses our sin; with him nothing is wasted. That's why the prophet Joel promised that the Lord would even "restore the years that the locust has eaten". That is especially good news for those who feel that they have totally misspent their lives or feel that they are right outside of God's will. Perhaps you feel you married the wrong person; perhaps you rejected a call to missionary work years ago; or maybe you frittered your days away in rebellion and disobedience. Well, I've got news for you! Bring it all to the Lord – lay the mess of your past at his feet and see what he can do. Think for a moment and look at the testimony which Scripture bears to this truth.

Do you remember the story of Samson, who ended up blind and in chains because of his folly? He completely missed the way, but even at the end, as he turned back to God, the Lord used him right there where he was. In the temple of Dagon, he slew more Philistines in his dying moments than in the whole of the rest of his life put together. And what about the dying thief? You can't be much closer to death than he was when he turned to Jesus. He had only minutes left; how could God possibly use him? Yet his story has touched millions over the last 2,000

The Forgiveness Equation

years. Who knows? He may prove to have been one of the most effective evangelists of all time. Certainly the greatest crime ever committed by humanity, the guilt of which we all share, was the nailing of the Prince of Peace to that cruel cross. We rejected the one who came to save us, but as we seek forgiveness for this most profane and barbarous act, it becomes our salvation!

Have you ever dared to think what would have happened if we had not crucified Jesus? I know it's a hypothetical question, but it is true that if he had not died there could have been no forgiveness. At the very height of our sinfulness God manifested his love towards us through the blood of his Son. Truly, the depths of his grace cannot be plumbed by the human mind. We can only stand amazed, looking out across the vast ocean of his love. Without any doubt he is the God of all grace. William Booth, founder of the Salvation Army, captures this awe-inspiring picture in the first two verses of his well-known hymn:

> *O boundless salvation! Deep ocean of love,*
> *O fulness of mercy, Christ brought from above,*
> *The whole world redeeming, so rich and so free,*
> *Now flowing for all men, come, roll over me!*
>
> *My sins they are many, their stains are so deep,*
> *And bitter the tears of remorse that I weep;*
> *But useless is weeping; thou great crimson sea,*
> *Thy waters can cleanse me, come, roll over me!*

Read: Joel 2:23-27; Romans 5:15-21.

Pray: Look to Jesus to give you a glimpse into his heart so that you can see how incredible his grace has been in the face of your particular history. Give him your past and

There's no waste with grace!

trust him to turn the darkness into light, and in his own inimitable way and time, to use even what you're ashamed of for his glory and the blessing of others. Worship him for his control over every aspect of your life, past, present and future!

16
Now grace is yours to give!

Peter came to Jesus and asked, "Lord, how many times shall I forgive my brother when he sins against me? Up to seven times?"

Matthew 18:21

Jesus had been teaching his disciples about relationships and how to live in harmony together. Peter had quickly grasped the importance of forgiveness, and moved as always by impulse and enthusiasm, popped his question to Jesus. I do love Peter and his willingness to make a fool of himself. There is a kind of naivety in him. It seems that no matter how badly wrong he is or how often he's proved to be wrong, he's always ready to jump in with both feet once again. I can identify with him. I too have an almost indomitable belief that I'm going to be right which has proved to be my undoing time and time again. But Jesus loved Peter and dealt with him patiently. I often wonder whether we would have ever heard some of Jesus' wisdom if Peter had not been there as a sort of catalyst.

In this matter of how many times to forgive, Peter did have reason for his optimism. I understand that at that time

Now grace is yours to give!

the rabbis taught that one should forgive three times. Even in some Jewish families today, if a member fails in business the others will rally round to give them up to three chances to prove themselves. In Bible terms, three is a good number, as it indicates completeness. So Peter went considerably further in suggesting seven times. No doubt some of those standing by and listening gasped at his generosity. Indeed seven, as a biblical number, speaks of perfection. Surely no one could demand more than that. Then Jesus replied, "I tell you, not seven times, but seventy-seven times." And that's according to the New International Bible; other versions tell us that the number is seventy times seven!

Either way, Jesus utterly blew away their tiny concepts and put forgiveness into an entirely different league. He was talking about infinity! No one who had any kind of heart for or understanding of forgiveness could find it in them to keep records that long. Paul confirms this in 1 Corinthians 13:5 when he states that love "keeps no record of wrongs". The simple fact is that we are called to minister the same quality of grace that we've received. It's amazing grace which came to us, and amazing grace is what we're expected to pass on. And that's not at all surprising, as it lines up with what the Scripture teaches in other areas. For example, we are called to be holy as God is holy; we are also told that we will be judged by the same judgment with which we judge. This latter promise is, I find, a real incentive to mercy!

You see, it's not that God is wagging his finger in our faces like a frustrated earthly parent calling for British fairplay amongst his children. His request for us to forgive to infinity comes against the background of the world's most unbelievable offer – "You give me your sin and death and I'll give you my righteousness and life!" The gift of infinite grace demands that we minister infinite grace to others. The reason for this is that the gift carries with it the ability to minister in

The Forgiveness Equation

just that way, so long as we choose to receive and walk in its power. Jesus illustrates this pointedly by telling the parable of the unmerciful servant. This man owes his master ten thousand talents, which in today's terms is probably around £6 million. Having been unconditionally forgiven for this massive debt, which is completely beyond his ability to pay, he finds a fellow servant who owes him a mere £10, and throws him into prison. When the master hears of this, he hands the unmerciful servant over to the jailers, who are to torture him until he clears the debt in full. Of course, once he is in prison, with his earning power lost, his chance of repaying what he owes is gone forever.

How can we, who are so undeserving of mercy, withhold mercy from those who have sinned against us? Our debt to the Lord is beyond measure and is not to be compared to what is owed to us. As we comprehend the magnitude of God's grace extended to us in Christ Jesus, we can only stand speechless in his presence and freely release all those who have sinned against us. This does not make what they have done right, but we can fully trust him to work out the implications of this. He has pledged himself to see justice brought to bear where his principles of mercy are spurned.

Read: Matthew 18:21-35.

Pray: Wait before the Lord Jesus and entreat him to create in you a habit of forgiveness. Cooperate with him and pray that your understanding of his grace to you increases to the point that forgiveness becomes second nature. Let thankfulness and appreciation of his goodness be your constant companions.

17
If . . .

My dear children, I write this to you so that you will not sin. But if anybody does sin, we have one who speaks to the Father in our defence – Jesus Christ, the Righteous One. He is the atoning sacrifice for our sins, and not only for ours but also for the sins of the whole world.

1 John 2:1-2

You don't have to be a professor of the Greek language to know that "if" does not mean "when". And you don't need to be a professor of English to know that there is a great deal of difference between the meanings of the words "if" and "when". Yet, for the majority of Christians, it seems that this distinction has not really been grasped. Generally, we have much more faith for the inevitability of sin in our lives than we do for the possibility of righteousness. Thus we live in what my friend Gerald Coates calls "the endless mess-up, wash-up process". Such Christians are trapped in the repetitive cycle of sinning, confessing, repenting and receiving forgiveness, and are forever taken up with their own failure. This merry-go-round (or rather,

The Forgiveness Equation

misery-go-round) has been created by the enemy to keep us from joyfully serving our Lord in holiness. It must be smashed so that all can be free from its trap.

Of course, none of us have achieved such perfection that we will never sin again. John, in the same letter, makes this clear when he says in verse 8 of chapter 1, "If we claim to be without sin, we deceive ourselves and the truth is not in us." None the less, he also makes it absolutely plain that "No-one who lives in him [Jesus] keeps on sinning," and that "no-one who continues to sin has either seen him [Jesus] or known him" (1 John 3:6). For those who are truly born of God, sin is no longer the norm – it is the exception. It is no longer "when" but "if". We are no longer slaves to sin, and although we may be prone to temptation, we are living under a new and different regime. Paul instructs the Colossian Christians, "Since, then, you have been raised with Christ, set your heart on things above" (Colossians 3:1), and he goes on in verse 5 to call them to "Put to death, therefore, whatever belongs to your earthly nature". Later, in verse 9, he encourages them with the words, "you have taken off your old self with its practices and have put on the new self, which is being renewed in knowledge in the image of its creator".

We have not been abandoned to work out our time under the control of our carnal passions, until we are rescued and whisked away to the heavenly mansion prepared for us in some ethereal space station. Jesus has placed within us the same Spirit which raised him from the dead, so that we can start to live our new lives right here in the present as an evidence that we are his children. Augustus Toplady expressed these sentiments in his famous hymn, "Rock of Ages". In the very first verse his faith in the effectiveness of Jesus' death cries out:

If . . .

*Let the water and the blood,
From thy riven side which flowed,
Be of sin the double cure,
Save me from its guilt and power.*

He realised that through the blood and water which poured out from Jesus' wounds came the potential not only for complete forgiveness from the guilt of all our sin, past, present and future, but also for strength to live clean and pure lives in the power of the Holy Spirit.

As we've seen, this call to holiness is not another more demanding and, therefore, more crushing law. It is not that the Ten Commandments of the Old Testament, which were totally impossible to keep, have now been replaced by the one hundred and ten commandments of the New Testament. Paul argues in Romans 10:4 that "Christ is the end of the law." Not that the law was bad; indeed, it was good, but it could not save us. The law could only point out our failure, and therefore, good though it was, it effectively separated us from God.

Now we have something infinitely better than the law. We have a resurrected Saviour who has come to dwell within us by the Holy Spirit. He enables us to live according to God's desires by strengthening us with his might in the inner man. So the first Pentecost, under Moses, brought us to Mount Sinai and gave us an external law in the form of cold tablets of stone, which broke us with their demands. But the second Pentecost, under Jesus, brought us to Mount Zion and gave us an internal helper, the Holy Spirit of God himself. There is no comparison between these two, for one says, "You must" and the other says, "You may"; one proves that "You can't" and the other establishes that "You can". Now, with Paul, we cry, "I have been crucified with Christ and I no longer live, but

The Forgiveness Equation

Christ lives in me. The life I live in the body, I live by faith in the Son of God, who loved me and gave himself for me. I do not set aside the grace of God, for if righteousness could be gained through the law, Christ died for nothing!" (Galatians 2:20-21).

Read: 1 John 2:1-11 & 3:1-10.

Pray: Do you have a bias towards the belief that you are *bound* to fail in your life as a Christian? Is your anticipation that you are *likely* to succumb to temptation? Do you tend to look for sin in your life, even when you are not conscious of having fallen? Think about the scriptures referred to in today's meditation, and if you discover a positive response to any of these questions, ask the Lord to give you a new hope and expectancy. As faith rises to the work Christ has already accomplished within you, look for strength to see practical changes in your attitude and daily walk.

18
Anoint the stone

Early the next morning Jacob took the stone he had placed under his head and set it up as a pillar and poured oil on top of it. He called that place Bethel.

Genesis 28:18

The tale of Jacob's dream is a familiar one to all those of us who attended Sunday School for any length of time, but I'm surprised that so few of those who know the story see any application to their own lives. Jacob, whose name means "Deceiver", had cheated his brother out of his father's blessing and, as a result, had to flee from his family and friends in fear of his life. On his first night away from home, lost and lonely, he took a stone for his pillow and slept. During the night he dreamt that he saw a stairway leading into God's presence. In his dream he saw the Lord, who also blessed him and promised never to leave him. In the morning he awoke and was alone again. Although he had experienced the Lord in his dreams, his problems remained and he could see no practical solution. Nevertheless, he took the stone which had been his pillow,

The Forgiveness Equation

up-ended it as a pillar and anointed it with oil, naming it Bethel – the house of God.

I know that many of you, my readers, will identify with Jacob. You do have some knowledge of God but you are conscious that you have not lived with integrity as you should, and that the problems you face, to some extent at least, are of your own making. You feel lonely and afraid and are not at all sure what to do or where to go. Can I encourage you to follow Jacob's example? He could have chosen to sit around all night worrying; instead he took a hard, unyielding stone – a symbol of his difficulty – and determined to sleep on it. There, in rest, he met with God; no practical or material help was forthcoming, only promises and more promises. In the cold light of day he held fast to the word the Lord had given and anointed the stone, together with his problems, with oil. The oil speaks of true spiritual worship, which Jacob offered to the Lord as he made vows to him. So that rock became the first step in the staircase into God's presence, or perhaps the first stone in the temple that was to be Bethel – God's house for him and his descendants.

Jesus was spoken of as a "stumbling-stone", a "rock of offence", and also a "foundation stone". He was a stone which could be rejected or one upon which a house could be built. Peter, in his first letter, says, "Now to you who believe, this stone is precious. But to those who do not believe' [it is] 'A stone that causes men to stumble and a rock that makes them fall'" (1 Peter 2:7-8). The way that we respond to the problems which the Lord allows to come across our paths determines whether we ascend into his presence and, like David, "dwell in his house forever", or whether we build and step down into a dungeon of despair and despondency. The difficulties we face as believers can provide a foundation which we treasure and

Anoint the stone

build into blessing; alternatively, we can despise those difficulties and allow them to become a curse to us.

In the fellowship of which I was a part for over twenty years, we had four couples who each lost a baby. In every case they anointed their stones and allowed their experiences to bring them closer to God. There was Gerry, who came home from a shopping trip to find her baby dead in her pram. She and her husband Bob fought their way to the feet of Jesus and discovered God's love in their moment of deepest need. We were awakened one morning by banging on our front door. It was our dear friend Anita. She was beside herself, because Nicola, her four-month-old daughter, had died in the night. Anita and her husband Ian found grace to walk through the darkness and have been able to strengthen others who face similar tragedies. Mike and Hilary's beautiful baby daughter was born with spinabifida and was destined to live only a short time, but Jesus helped them make those months a time of tremendous blessing and enrichment. What a triumph for them both and for the Lord that friends and neighbours alike saw God at work in their tragedy. Then there was Meg and Brian, whose little daughter Margaret "died" after surgery for a deformed heart. Though clinically dead, she was kept alive, and for six long weeks they cried out to Jesus to take their child home. Through all the tears their testimony was that the joy of the Lord was their strength.

The truly terrible tragedies are not these stories but those of others who have permitted prosperity rather than pain to turn them from God. The rich young ruler, the successful salesman, the pastor of the largest church, the beautiful wife who lacked nothing, the intelligent teenager – I could go on. The world is full of people upon whom life has heaped its blessings, and yet they have no sense of

The Forgiveness Equation

needing God. Paul summed it all up when he told the Philippian saints, "I know what it is to be in need, and I know what it is to have plenty. I have learned the secret of being content in any and every situation . . . I can do everything through him who gives me strength" (Philippians 4:12-13).

Read: Genesis 28:10-22; 1 Peter 2:4-10.

Pray: I am appealing here to those who have had devastating experiences of pain, bereavement or rejection. For some of you, these situations and circumstances will have come suddenly and unexpectedly; for others they are, at least partly, due to your own folly. In either case you are likely to be tempted to retreat from your faith in the Lord or from your relationships with others, particularly from those who you feel are responsible for your hurt. Seek God's help to look beyond the traumas, anointing them with the oil of the Holy Spirit's presence, even through your tears. Ultimately you will see that which you anoint become the very place of blessing and fruitfulness.

19
Learning from others

. . . and a little child shall lead them.

Isaiah 11:6

I'm a family man. I've been married for well over thirty years. Christine and I have brought up five children; all are now mature adults. We have seven grandchildren at the time of writing, most of whom have lived with us together with their parents for at least a part of their lives. Our two eldest grandchildren, Victoria and Joshua, with their mum and dad, have lived with us since they were born, which for Victoria was in 1980. Anyone who has, with God's help, survived the rigours and joys of this kind of life in a society where the family is under severe attack, must have learned something. I have learned much, mostly from my offspring and theirs.

Matthew, my eldest son, was about eight at the time. It was during the years when the old currency and the new decimal currency were happily coexisting in the overlap. Matthew came home from school as usual for lunch, and, being in full-time Christian ministry then, I was home for

The Forgiveness Equation

lunch too, as most of my work was in the evenings and at weekends. Matthew looked a little concerned. Like his father before him, he was not the brightest boy in the school. Once he'd got something he'd got it, but sometimes it took him quite a while to get it! The subject giving him problems was maths, and the area he just couldn't grasp was pounds, shillings and pence. "Never fear lad, your old dad will help you. Let's have a look at it while mum rustles up some lunch." An innocent enough scenario? A loving father drawing alongside his small son to give him a helping hand. But we were just about to walk into a minefield!

I explained clearly to my confused son that there were twelve pennies in one shilling, twenty shillings in one pound and, therefore, two hundred and forty pennies in a pound. It seemed simple enough to me, but, of course, he'd heard about half-pennies and farthings. By this time Christine had let us know that lunch was almost ready. It was at this point that I made by big mistake. "Okay, love," I said with confidence, "don't worry; I'll just make sure Matthew's got this, then we'll be with you." So we went over it again, dealing with the ha'pennies and farthings. Matthew's confusion grew with my determination to make him understand. "Lunch is on the table." Christine's voice came through from the dining room with a slightly threatening note creeping in. "Darling, give us a couple more minutes. We are going to get this before we have lunch," I said firmly.

So we covered the ground once more, but sensing that he was rapidly becoming the centre of a developing storm, my son just couldn't concentrate. "Dinner is getting cold!" Christine snapped, but I completely ignored her. All my attention was directed at Matthew, who was now unable to hear anything I was saying. I went over the facts

Learning from others

yet again, but it was useless; there was fear in Matthew's eyes. My temper boiled over and I lashed out, hitting the boy around the head – a thing I should never have done. He looked up at me with his large hazel eyes; they filled with tears and he began to cry. Then, through his quivering lips, came the words which put me to shame and broke the situation wide open: "Jesus, please help me," he cried.

Well, that was all that was needed. Matthew had touched the Lord for the whole family. I cracked completely and asked his forgiveness, which he freely gave. Christine and I were reconciled, and the other kids looked at one another and breathed a huge sigh of relief. The words of the prophet were fulfilled – a little child had taken the lead and the lion and the lamb were able to lie down together in peace. As Jesus said when he set a child in their midst, "I tell you the truth, unless you change and become like little children, you will never enter the kingdom of heaven."

Read: Isaiah 11:6-9; Matthew 18:1-6 & 19:13-14.

Pray: Ask your heavenly Father to forgive you for anything you may have done to harm children – your own or others. Ask forgiveness for the terrible sin our nation is committing against the unborn child. Pray for the children of our churches, for the young of our land. Ask the Lord to turn the hearts of the children to their parents. Pray for our schools and for all who work with children.

20
Forgiving and releasing

There was a man who had two sons. The younger one said to his father, "Father, give me my share of the estate." So he divided his property between them.

Luke 15:11-12

So began one of the best known and most loved of Jesus' parables – the story of the prodigal son. I'm sure the reason for its popularity is because so many of us can identify with that young man. As one who seriously backslid and experienced my heavenly Father's joyful reception and welcome home, I most certainly can. For some years after the commencement of our work in East London, Christine put a considerable amount of effort into the development of a mime and movement group. One piece which rapidly became a classic was a short production of this moving story. There were no words, only narration in the form of a song. The scenes, acted out between each verse, vividly translated the tale into the modern idiom.

The climax, was, of course, the return. The father was depicted as always longing, waiting and watching. In fact,

Forgiving and releasing

one word was used in the play. As the boy came to his senses he cried out in anguish, "Father!" At this point – even when the play was performed before thousands in the Royal Albert Hall – a hush came over the audience and you could have heard a pin drop. Then the lad began the slow and painful journey home. As he came into the father's view, there was a moment of hesitation, each looking to see what was written in the eyes of the other before they ran full tilt into one another's arms. Oh, the crying, the laughing, the hugging as they swung one another around in their joy! No matter how many times I watched this finale, I always wept, because I was that son.

As the years passed and I became more involved in Christian work, I discovered that the parable was not simply about a lost son, but about two brothers. At times I felt hardness of heart and jealousy towards those who, in my view, did not deserve God's blessing. I began to take God's grace for granted and lost sight of all that was mine in Christ. The church is full of such "elder brothers". They should set an example, but are actually the cause of many young people turning away, rejecting the self-righteousness and hypocrisy which they come to equate with church life. In those periods I forgot the joy of serving Jesus for who he was and worked out of a false sense of duty and a feeling that I needed to earn my keep. This can become really dangerous. At least when we are obviously backslidden we know it, but when we're still working at our Father's home with a cold heart, we may not realise just how far away we have really wandered. But the story had one further lesson for me.

John Junior is the baby of our family, even though he's in his mid-twenties. He's the one of our five children who is most like me, and, no doubt for this very reason, he caused me a great deal of frustration. His school reports read like a carbon copy of mine: "Could do better if he tried harder"; "This young man has brains but won't use them"; and so on. What's more, he was a leader, like his dad, and somehow school had never found a way of utilising the kind of skills he and I possessed, and we both found ourselves alienated and considered to be rebellious. "Why can't he learn from my mistakes?" I demanded from Christine. But she only replied with another question: "Why should he learn from his dad any more than you learned from yours?" Then one day, when he was sixteen, he did something which really angered me, probably because it was just the kind of thing I would have done at his age. My temper boiled over and we were into physical confrontation before I realised what was happening.

I grabbed him around the throat and, big though he was, threw him to the floor. I put my knee on his chest and reached out for the baseball bat on his dresser. I'd bought it for him when we were holidaying in the USA a couple of years before as a symbol of our friendship. I waved it threateningly over his head. He matched my glare with a stare and said exactly what I would have said to my father in a similar situation: "Go on then – 'it me!" I threw down the bat in horror as I faced the reality of what I was doing, and ran into my own bedroom crying out to God for help. Immediately the Lord reminded me that all that week he had been trying to get through to me that it was time for me to release John and give him his freedom. However, I had fought against such action, as I feared that it would mean him going away from the Lord as I had when my father died and left me without adequate authority at the same age. So, I had been the prodigal son, and I also knew what it was to be in the position of the elder brother, but now the Lord was asking that I share, in a small way, the

Forgiving and releasing

fellowship of his suffering by discovering what it was like to be the prodigal father!

For a brief moment I struggled, but then I knew what I must do. I went back to John and asked his forgiveness for my wrongdoing. I explained that he was to be a free man and responsible for his own actions. I promised I would never nag him again, only offer my advice if it was wanted. I told him that he could live his own life and only asked that he respected his parents' views. Our home was his for as long as he wanted to share it. We embraced and wept on one another's shoulders as he freely forgave me. Since that day we have been true friends, enjoying one another's company and doing many things together. John is deeply sympathetic to our faith but at present does not share it, at least in the same way. Almost daily I stand, like the father in the parable, watching and waiting for him to make the journey back, which I know one day he will, just as I did.

This experience has given me a deeper insight into the Father's heart. I understand a little more how he feels in his relationship to fallen humanity. He cares for us deeply, but will not break the delicate cord of love by impairing our free will. Thus he ensures that when we do come home, it's because we choose to, not because we've been manipulated or blackmailed into it. John knew only too well where I stood in regard to my faith. It was not a time for sermons but a time for releasing in the natural and holding on in spirit. I could only do that because I had learned to trust my heavenly Father's judgement more than my own and was convinced that he cared more about my son's future than I ever did. You can do the same with your teenager, or your unconverted husband, or whoever it is that you are grasping to yourself in an effort to bring them to Jesus. Lovingly let go and let God.

The Forgiveness Equation

Read: Luke 15:11-32.

Pray: Pray for strength and wisdom to forgive and release those dearest to you who you may be holding on to. If you have sought to pressurise or manipulate them you will need to ask their forgiveness and verbally set them free. Obviously, with young people and teenagers in your family, timing is of the essence. Releasing does not mean you become passive, just that your activity moves from the physical into the spiritual realm of prayer and intercession for them.

21
Power to forgive!

Again Jesus said, "Peace be with you! As the Father has sent me, I am sending you." And with that he breathed on them and said, "Receive the Holy Spirit. If you forgive anyone his sins, they are forgiven: if you do not forgive them, they are not forgiven."

John 20:21-23

I almost fear to draw attention to a passage like this, which has caused such controversy amongst God's people over the centuries. Nevertheless, how can we afford to overlook such powerful words when considering the subject of forgiveness? Personally, I do not believe that these promises were given to the apostles alone or to some élite grouping within the church, but rather to all believers. Today, Jesus is sending us in the same way that the Father sent him and just as he sent his followers 2,000 years ago. We have the same message of good news for the poor as Jesus had; we can also have the same character, walking in holiness; and we can have the same power at work within us. The key which opens up to us the ability to pronounce God's forgiveness is the Holy Spirit.

The Forgiveness Equation

Only Jesus has the right to forgive sin, and he earned that right by paying the very highest price. Nothing less than his life would satisfy God's immutable justice – an eye for an eye, a tooth for a tooth and a life for a life. He settled our accounts in full and won the prerogative to open our prison and declare to us, "Your many sins are forgiven." He is no longer here in the flesh to preach and heal and proclaim God's acceptance, but nevertheless he has a body. We, those who are redeemed through his precious blood, are his hands, his feet and his mouthpiece. Paul emphatically states in 1 Corinthians 12:27: "Now you are the body of Christ, and each one of you is a part of it." Furthermore, the words of Jesus endorse this. Having announced to all men, "I am the light of the world" (John 9:5), in his Sermon on the Mount in Matthew's Gospel he tells us, "You are the light of the world" (5:14). Again, as if to make it absolutely clear, in John 14:12 Jesus underlines what he has been saying: "I tell you the truth, anyone who has faith in me will do what I have been doing. He will do even greater things than these, because I am going to the Father." So, how can this be? By what means can we continue the work of Jesus today?

Before Jesus gave his disciples the ability to forgive sins he breathed on them and said, "Receive the Holy Spirit." In fact, they did not receive the Spirit at that moment, nor did they begin their ministry at that point. It was later, in the upper room, when the day of Pentecost had fully come, that the Holy Spirit fell upon them and filled them to overflowing. After this experience they began to function and continued the ministry which Jesus began. Ever since that day it has been the responsibility of the Holy Spirit to reproduce Christ's character and power in the hearts and lives of those who yield themselves to him. So it is that Christ is born, comes to maturity and lives through

Power to forgive!

his church. We have authority in his name to preach the gospel, heal the sick and proclaim forgiveness of sins, but only in and through the power of the Holy Spirit. As the first Christians needed their Pentecost, so also do we. It is by the Holy Spirit alone and through the gifts he imparts that we can deliver the full, undiluted message of the lordship of Christ which releases God's power to save sinners.

How important it is for us all to hear those words, "Your many sins are forgiven." Especially in an age where cults flourish which tell us, on the one hand, that we have no sin, and on the other that we have to work for our salvation. Only the truth of God, proclaimed in the power of the Spirit, will set men free. Knowing how God views sin, how he punishes the unrepentant and how he freely forgives all who come to him, is vital if people are to be clearly born of the Spirit. Half-truths leave men groping in darkness and confusion, and the church has too often been guilty of aiding and abetting the enemy in his quest to keep folk in that state. Thank the Lord that more and more of his people are opening their lives up to the Holy Spirit and are receiving the power to minister forgiveness and healing in Christ's name and by his command, "All authority in heaven and on earth has been given to me. Therefore go . . ."

Read: John 20:19-23; 1 Corinthians 12:12-27; Matthew 5:13-16.

Pray: Come confidently into the Lord's presence and beseech him to send the Holy Spirit in greater power into your life, so that you might be an agent for his grace and gifts. Meditate on the fact that you are a chosen vessel, set apart to bear his image; a channel through which his love

The Forgiveness Equation

and judgement can flow into the world. Respond to the Spirit as he creates faith in your heart and determine to act on that impartation. Do things you have never done before in bringing healing and forgiveness to those who are open and are receiving Jesus and his message of truth through you.

22
Confession is nine-tenths . . .

If you confess with your mouth, "Jesus is Lord," and believe in your heart that God raised him from the dead, you will be saved.
Romans 10:9

If we confess our sins, he is faithful and just and will forgive us our sins and purify us from all unrighteousness.
1 John 1:9

Therefore confess your sins to each other and pray for each other so that you may be healed.
James 5:16

If there's a law of forgiveness, it seems to me that confession is nine-tenths of it. We've seen how important it is for us to hear God's pronouncement concerning his attitude to our sin. It is also necessary to him to hear from us that we appreciate the error of our ways and that we value his salvation. Many people consider Christianity to be a private and personal thing, and they are offended at the thought of testimony or public confession. Yet Jesus made it abundantly plain that open acknowledgement of our relationship to him and of our break with the past is an

The Forgiveness Equation

essential part, and even an evidence, of our new life. So much of what Jesus did and so many of the responses he called for were in full public view. He called is disciples in public, healed the sick on the street and dealt with the sins of ordinary folk and religious people out in the open air.

Jesus cautioned the crowds about the hypocrisy of hiding their sins under a cloak of religiosity and warned them that "There is nothing concealed that will not be disclosed, or hidden that will not be made known." He went even further, saying, "What you have said in the dark will be heard in the daylight, and what you have whispered in the ear in the inner rooms will be proclaimed from the roofs" (Luke 12:2-3). Proverbs 28:13 confirms this wisdom: "He who conceals his sins does not prosper, but whoever confesses and renounces them finds mercy." David the psalmist also understood this truth well and wrote in Psalm 32, "Blessed is he whose transgressions are forgiven, whose sins are covered . . . I said, 'I will confess my transgressions to the Lord' – and you forgave the guilt of my sin." Speaking out the truth to the Lord, to one another and even to Satan (as Jesus did during his temptation) releases God's power into our lives. Truly, confession is good for the soul.

Tragically, we have preached what C. T. Studd called a "confectionery gospel" which produces "chocolate soldiers" and they melt when the heat is on. We have offered people "sweets" as an incentive to come to Christ. We have told them that if they receive Jesus, they'll have peace, joy, healing and a ticket to heaven, when the truth of the matter is that in this life we may have tribulation, hardship and even persecution, but in the next, life eternal. Is it any wonder that many Christians are disappointed and disillusioned with Christianity? It has not met their expectations; no one told them that making Jesus Lord might mean sacrifice and suffering. No one called them to take up their cross and

Confession is nine-tenths . . .

follow Jesus through trials and testings, with the ultimate reward being a share in his glory. So we must understand that there is no place for secret believers. We must audibly acknowledge our sins and lift Jesus up visibly in our lives. In the words of Isaac Watts' old hymn:

> *I'm not ashamed to own my Lord,*
> *Or to defend his cause.*
> *Maintain the honour of his word,*
> *The glory of his cross.*

Obviously, confessing Christ publicly or confessing our sins to one another demands wisdom and sensitivity. Arrogantly thrusting our testimony down folk's throats or preaching at them is not what we're talking about. Nor are we required to pour out the morbid, gory details of our misdemeanours into the ears and minds of all and sundry – this may lead us or them into greater sin. But a healthy openness and a willingness to acknowledge our weaknesses, at least in general terms, will lead us into a proper dependency on the body of Christ and will ensure that we receive loving discipline and support. Therefore confess your sins and cover one another with love, honesty and forgiveness.

Read: Romans 10:8-13; Luke 12:1-12; Psalm 32.

Pray: There are three areas where confession is necessary and helpful: confession before God, confession to principalities and powers and confession to one another. Ask the Holy Spirit to guide you and be ready to speak out as he leads. This will certainly involve declaration in your prayer time, public testimony to individuals in your church and confession to those with whom you are involved in life and fellowship.

23
Sorry – you can't blame Grandma

The soul who sins is the one who will die. The son will not share the guilt of the father, nor will the father share the guilt of the son.

Ezekiel 18:20

There has been a trend in modern psychiatry to place the responsibility for our reactions on anyone or anything other than ourselves. We are the products of our environment. We are inherently good; it is just that we have been damaged or conditioned by our circumstances. If things had been different, we would have been different. So my weaknesses are nothing to do with me – it was Grandma. She locked me in a cupboard or dropped me on my head, and I've never been the same since. Of course, there is some truth in this theory. A bad background can most certainly have bad effects, just as a good one may serve us well. But this is by no means a foregone conclusion.

The Bible also supports the idea, and we read in the third of the Ten Commandments that "God is a jealous God, punishing the children for the sin of the fathers to the

Sorry – you can't blame Grandma

the third and fourth generation of those who hate me" (Exodus 20:5). Even a superficial study of our family traits and our national characteristics will reveal that we do maintain and reproduce the weaknesses of our forebears. Amazingly enough, baby batterers are likely to produce baby batterers, and those who lie often breed liars, and so on. The effects of sin are like a disease which is passed on, whereas righteousness is a gift from God. Nevertheless, there are those who study the brain and our responses who will tell us that even the most demented maniac, seemingly governed totally by external forces beyond himself, actually makes a choice a split-second before taking action. Yes, we need to be sympathetic and understand the pressures and temptations which plague men and the traits which they inherit, but at the end of it all each one of us will stand before God and will be held accountable for what he has chosen to do or failed to do.

There is a delicate balance between the need for deliverance from the effects of our past and accepting responsibility for our sins and throwing ourselves on God for mercy. None of us can finally hide behind the excuse that "The devil made me do it." There may well be a demon of laziness, but he has no power unless we give him ground. It is true that we become the slaves of sin, but that is because we practise it and yield ourselves to its lure and corrupting influence. Trying to plumb the depths of this mystery has kept theologians in business for centuries. Where are the limits of man's ability to choose, and how does this blend with the all-knowing sovereignty of God? The truth of this matter is beyond the grasp of our finite minds. But Scripture does provide examples which can help us to see how we should respond to the Lord.

The story of the demoniac recorded in Mark 5 is a case in point. Here was a man so heavily demonised that no one

The Forgiveness Equation

had been able to control him. Even when he was bound with chains, his supernatural strength tore them apart and broke the irons on his feet. But in spite of the driving force within him, when he saw Jesus, he ran and worshipped at his feet. It is significant that there are three instances of healing in this chapter, and in each case the recipient of the miracle was found worshipping at the feet of Jesus. The demoniac is one case, the woman with the issue of blood is another and the centurion whose daughter had died is a third. These three manifestations of Jesus' power demonstrate his complete authority over evil in the lives of those who come and bow before him. In this single day's ministry he conquered the trinity of darkness by defeating the devil, disease and death itself.

So, it is my understanding – and I believe that Scripture supports it – that no matter how bound a person may be, deep within their being there is the potential to reach out to God if they have the desire. They may well need a miracle to set them free in order that they can love and serve the Lord, but when the opportunity presents itself they too can cry out for help, as multitudes of others have throughout this age of grace. Of course, this must be set against the commission, which those of us who are secure in Jesus' love carry, to constantly ask the Spirit to guide us to the lost and needy who are longing for a salvation and deliverance which they may be unaware even exists. We must follow in the footsteps of our Master, who obeyed his Father's leading, crossing the lake for the sake of a single, lonely, tormented soul. And we must always remember that we can do nothing to save ourselves, let alone anyone else, unless we cooperate with the Holy Spirit, who is anxious to draw all men to Jesus.

Read: Ezekiel 18; Colossians 3:1-17.

Sorry – you can't blame Grandma

Pray: Have you been dodging the issue of your sin by pushing the responsibility on to others or blaming your circumstances? Do you secretly believe that some are unable to respond to God even in the most minimal way? If either of these things is true, ask the Lord Jesus for a deeper understanding of how you can exercise your will and seek his intervention in your life. Cry out to him for faith to help others find their way to Jesus' feet and to the deliverance or healing which they need to set them on the road to victorious living.

24
Grounds for divorce

Do not give the devil a foothold.

Ephesians 4:27

. . . the prince of this world is coming. He has no hold on me . . .

John 14:30

A plane can dive and circle overhead, but to land it needs a runway. In order to gain access to a property, one needs a right of way. It is no different for Satan and his minions. He may shoot his fiery darts of scorn and temptation, but unless he has ground in our lives he has no right of entry. This is why we are cautioned not to give him so much as a foothold or, in climbing terms, a toehold in our lives. Watch the mountaineer search for the tiniest place to obtain a grip, and see how much he can accomplish with so little. Likewise, our enemy is always on the lookout for a crack or fracture in our defences so that he can find a way to control or manipulate us.

Jesus was aware that the devil was coming to seek to overthrow him, but he was confident that there was no place

Grounds for divorce

where he could get a hold. He had walked in holiness, keeping himself pure and untainted by the world in which he lived. He was totally dependent on his Father and attempted nothing without the heavenly stamp of approval. No wonder Satan became angry and frustrated and finally overstepped the mark, so that his own act of aggression became the means of his defeat. We don't have to fight the devil; all we are called to do is stand, and in the end he will overstretch himself, and the Lord will cause even evil to serve his purposes and work for our good.

Since we are children of God, Satan has no claim on our lives other than the ground we give him. If we allow him in to just one room he will occupy it, but he will never be satisfied until he has taken over our whole house like the squatter he is. His presence comes between us and God, cutting us off from our source of life and ultimately causing divorce. We have no ability to eject him apart from cooperating and working together with the Holy Spirit. But one person cooperating with him is a majority against which nothing can stand. James shares with us the simple answer in verse 7 of chapter 4 of his letter. By submitting our lives to God in the midst of our weakness, agreeing with him and accepting his scrutiny and his judgements, we will have the wherewithall to resist the devil and see the powers of darkness scamper away like frightened rabbits. The choice is ours; the question is, who are we going to yield to – Christ or the devil?

David and Saul were both kings in Israel; both had been set apart and anointed by God and both fell into serious sin by giving Satan ground. David stayed at home when he should have been at war, and so he fell foul of the tempter. Saul deliberately disobeyed the Lord, allowing greed to be his master in spite of all that God had given him. David submitted to God, accepting his judgement and forgiveness; but Saul chose to live in guilt, which eventually led him to

The Forgiveness Equation

take his own life. We cannot save ourselves, but by choosing Christ we become the masters of our own destiny. In Deuteronomy the Lord says, "See, I set before you today life and prosperity, death and destruction . . . Now choose life . . ." (30:15, 19).

In Colossians 3:5, on the foundation that we have been raised with Christ, Paul calls us to "Put to death, therefore, whatever belongs to your earthly nature." He then lists the kind of things he is talking about, to make sure we are in no doubt. Then he goes on, "Therefore, as God's chosen people, holy and dearly loved, clothe yourselves with compassion, kindness, humility, gentleness and patience" (verse 12). The risen Christ lives within each of us who have surrendered to him. He is the one who strengthens us and gives us the resolve to send Satan packing and put to death his works in our experience. He is the one who will live through us, manifesting his love and all the fruits of the Holy Spirit. With Paul, we too can say with confidence, "For to me, to live is Christ," and "I can do everything through him (Christ) who gives me strength" (Philippians 1:21 & 4:13). Let us take back the ground which Satan has claimed and allow nothing come between us and our relationship with Jesus. Let us give no ground for divorce.

Read: Ephesians 4:17-32; Deuteronomy 30:11-19.

Pray: Is the Holy Spirit bringing to your attention aspects of your life which give Satan an entrance into your experience, through which he can manipulate or control you in some way? These may be long-established habits or undealt-with areas which need to be brought out into the light. Ask for the Spirit's empowering to recognise these things and to choose the way of "life and prosperity", thus rejecting "death and destruction".

25
Men who heard from heaven

Therefore, since we are surrounded by such a great cloud of witnesses . . . Let us fix our eyes on Jesus, the author and perfecter of our faith.

Hebrews 12:1-2

Years ago, when I was starting out in my ministry, a book came my way the title of which intrigued me. It was called *Men Who Heard From Heaven*. I knew God was calling me and I thought that the stories of others whom the Lord had used might perhaps encourage and strengthen me, but the opposite was the case. Chapter after chapter told of men who had had amazing experiences with God. Some had been visited by the Lord Jesus in person; others had angels appear to them whilst they were praying; some raised the dead or at least performed many mighty miracles which confirmed their calling. As I read on I became more and more depressed, wondering if I was mistaken in my belief that God wanted to use me. It was not until the very last chapter, when I'd almost given up hope, that I read about one man whom I could identify with. He had seen no

The Forgiveness Equation

visions or lights in the sky, and he'd not performed any great miracles, but he knew that God had spoken to him deep within. He held fast to what God had said to him and he stepped out in faith to serve the Lord, trusting that inner witness of the Holy Spirit.

Some time after this I found myself reading Hebrews chapters 11 and 12, and I was struck by a remarkable similarity to the book I had read. Here was an incredible list of men and women who performed tremendous exploits, each one testifying to the greatness and the power of the Lord they served. All of this could have been quite intimidating if that was where it finished, but as chapter 11 closed I read about the "others". They were tortured, they faced jeers and floggings, they were stoned, they were sawn in two, they went about in skins, living in caves and holes in the ground – not exactly a success from a worldly perspective! But all were commended for their faith. As I read on into the beginning of chapter 12, the light suddenly went on.

All of these men and women – many of them heroes but some of them failures in human terms – were witnesses to something and someone else. They looked towards a kingdom age which would be ushered in by the Messiah for whom they longed. They all died without having seen the promise, but for us he is here – Jesus is alive! In a flash it all fell into place. I was not to concentrate on the great cloud of witnesses, relevant though their lives and testimonies were; rather I was called to fix my eyes on Jesus, the author and finisher of my faith. Everything given to us by God should point and direct us towards Jesus. If we lock our gaze on him we will not be drawn aside. Unfortunately, at times we spend too long looking at others, and instead of being an inspiration and encouragement to us, they become a diversion or even a threat.

Men who heard from heaven

When we take our eyes off the Lord and keep them focused on men – even Godly men – things start to go wrong. Firstly, if they are especially gifted, we will be impressed or intimidated. Either way, we will find ourselves becoming impotent and ineffective, and we may well cause them to stumble by putting them on pedestals or by being jealous of them. Secondly, if we see their feet of clay, we may find pride springing up in our hearts as we thank God that we are not as they are. When we see the strengths or weaknesses of others, we should always turn our attention to Jesus. On the one hand we can praise him for the diversity of his creation and thank him for those he is using in such powerful ways, and on the other hand we can pray for the ones who are struggling with temptation and failure.

When Elisha, the young prophet in the making, was called to follow Elijah, he was full of zeal and demanded a double portion of the Spirit which rested on his master. He was told that this special blessing would be his, provided he saw Elijah when he was taken from him. You can imagine how the young man kept his mentor firmly in his sights every second of the day, hardly daring to blink lest he would find him gone when he opened his eyes. But he saw the chariots of fire and witnessed the whirlwind which carried Elijah up to heaven. The mantle of the teacher fell upon the student, who went back in the power of the same Spirit. The disciples too managed to keep their eyes on their Master and saw him carried up into the clouds. Soon after, the power which had been so clearly seen upon Jesus fell upon them. That power is still falling today on all those who fix their eyes on the Lord, but we are called to watch for his coming with the clouds. So do not measure yourself against or compare yourself with others; the Scripture warns that this practice is unwise.

The Forgiveness Equation

Rather:

> *Turn your eyes upon Jesus,*
> *Look full in his wonderful face,*
> *And the things of earth will grow strangely dim,*
> *In the light of his glory and grace.*

Read: Hebrews 11:32-12:3; 2 Kings 2:1-14; 2 Corinthians 10:12-18.

Pray: If you have been guilty of comparing yourself to others or looking to men rather than the Lord, recognise the danger of this and ask for his forgiveness. Begin to consciously turn your thoughts and gaze to Jesus and pray for strength to make this a daily habit. Pray for those who you have wronged, either by magnifying their value or despising their faults.

26
Have you forgiven God? And what about his church?

In all this, Job did not sin by charging God with wrongdoing.
Job 1:22

Christ loved the church and gave himself up for her . . .
Ephesians 5:25

It may sound strange to some people to ask the question, "Have you forgiven God?" Perhaps it may not sound quite so strange to ask, "Have you forgiven his church?" The truth is that there are many Christians who cannot face the reality that they carry a grudge against God. In their minds they know he is holy and beyond reproach, but something in their experiences tells them differently, so they end up living in lies. They publicly sing of his goodness, but secretly believe he is unfair or unjust in some way towards them. The church, on the other hand, has been the cause of much pain, and anyone who has been a Christian for any length of time will have suffered as a result of being part of

The Forgiveness Equation

the church. I have heard more than once remarks such as "The Lord is fantastic, but I don't think much of his church!" and "I love Jesus, but I can't stand Christians!" The fact which we must come to terms with is that Jesus and his church are one. The church actually is his body; if we disclaim one we scorn the other.

Of all those who could feel justified in feeling that God had let them down, Job must feature near the top of the list. He lost everything he possessed, including family and wealth. I was introduced to Job as a young Christian. One night I was having difficulty sleeping, as I had some kind of nervous itch. Every time I got comfortable I itched, so I scratched and settled down again, only to itch somewhere else. In the end I rose from my bed and went into the bathroom and towelled myself with the roughest towel I could find. It was bliss! I returned to bed but within seconds I was itching again. Finally I gave up and went into the lounge, where I read the first seventeen chapters of Job. I guess I thought I would find comfort in reading about someone who was much worse off than me. From that time on I often read about Job, and he has proved to be a faithful friend and companion.

At first I was quite surprised, because he was not your standard haloed saint. I had read elsewhere of "the patience of Job" and expected to find a mild-mannered, uncomplaining, peaceable kind of chap. Not so – he let it all hang out. He moaned and groaned and argued and questioned, but never once did he falsely accuse the Lord. It was just that he could not understand what was going on. Neither his wife nor his friends were able to help, as they were less spiritual than he. Only the young man Elihu could silence the flow of Job's self-justification long enough for God to speak, and finally he did. Not with slating words of condemnation, but with reason and mild

Have you forgiven God? And what about his church?

rebuke. For God used all the trials which Satan had brought upon Job to reveal his grace – and not grace alone, but full restoration and double blessing.

While it is true that God is beyond reproach and has never done anything which needs forgiving, he can cope with our frustrations and our confusion. Like Job and David of old, we need to pour them out and vent them all upon him. Don't be afraid to ask even the haunting questions: "Why did you let it happen, Lord?"; "Why did you take him or her Jesus?"; "What did I do to deserve this treatment?"; "Are you really there at all?" – and oh, so many more. Then, when all the pain has surfaced, God will speak. He may not give you all the answers, but his voice and presence will suffice until the time comes when all will be revealed. However, the church is a different matter.

The church is made up of folks just like you and me – hurting people, wounded people, over-confident people and people who are in the learning process. They've not yet arrived but, believe it or not, most of them really are on the way. They will not always be in a position to give us what we need, when we need it. And, what's more, we will not always be in a position to receive, for one reason or another. There is absolutely no doubt that if we come to the church with wrong expectations, we will be greatly disappointed. But if we come with a serving heart, we may well be surprised at what we find. Our attitude towards the church needs to be that of Jesus, who loved her and gave himself for her. In spite of all her shortcomings, she is the instrument through which God has chosen to work. Like it or not, we cannot reach our goals without her. We would all do well to ponder the advice given by the old sage to the young man who sought the "perfect church". "When you

The Forgiveness Equation

find it," the sage warned the young man, "whatever you do, do not join it, lest you ruin it again!"

Read: Job 34:1-15 & 42:1-6, 10-11; Ephesians 5:25-33.

Pray: If you have become aware of situations or circumstances in your past for which you blame God, or if you doubt his love because of events which have overtaken you, begin to pour out your hurts to the Lord. Let him hear your questions and stay with him until you feel the Holy Spirit beginning to minister to you. You will see God's perfection in a new light as you have a revelation of his appreciation of your pain. Then you will have the power to ask for pardon and cleansing. Think about the church and ask the Lord to help you see things from his perspective. Determine with his aid to become a servant rather than a critic. Forgive those who have wronged you, particularly leaders, and accept responsibility for your own insensitivity to the needs of others. Pray for the church worldwide in all its diversity.

27
The unacceptable gift

If you are offering your gift at the altar and there remember that your brother has something against you, leave your gift there in front of the altar. First go and be reconciled to your brother; then come and offer your gift.

Matthew 5:23-24

Under the new covenant, secured for us through the blood of Jesus, we are no longer required to bring literal offerings to altars constructed in temples of stone. However, we are called to bring offerings of thanksgiving and praise into God's house, which is now built from the living stone of our lives and service. Now it is even more important for us to be in right relationships together within the church; if we are not, our worship is polluted. What's more, Paul, in Romans 12, directed us to "offer your bodies as living sacrifices, holy and pleasing to God," and advised us that "this is your spiritual act of worship". Therefore, since Christ is our sacrifice, there is no need for the blood of bulls or goats, or indeed for any other kind of external offering. And, as we are clean through the application

The Forgiveness Equation

his blood, we can place ourselves before the Lord to be used as he chooses. Nevertheless, it is necessary to keep ourselves pure and unspotted in our fellowship – otherwise we will quickly find that we are divided and ineffective.

After the decisive victory at Jericho, Joshua immediately sent a smaller company of men to take the city of Ai. The men of Ai were no match for the Israelites, but Joshua had failed to enquire of the Lord concerning this venture, and his army was routed. This defeat put him on his face before the Lord. He rent his garments and cried out to God, who pointed to sin in the camp. Step by step Joshua went about dealing with the problem. First, the tribes were brought before him, and Judah was taken; then the clans of Judah paraded, and the Zerahites were taken; then the families came one by one, and Zimri was taken; finally Zimri's family came one by one, and Achan was exposed as the one who had sinned. He was taken, with his household and all he possessed, to the valley of Achor, where they were stoned, burned and buried. A severe judgement which revealed how seriously God viewed deliberate and premeditated sin about which he had previously clearly warned them. The primary lesson which we must learn from this story is that when the people of God go into battle, they fight together as one man, sharing the victories and the defeats. The success of one is enjoyed by all, and the failure of one affects the welfare of all the others.

The fact is that we are not a group of individuals who occasionally do things together. We are the army of God and are expected to work in total harmony. Few Christians share a true feeling of common identity, and as a result there is little sense of responsibility or care for others, and loyalty is a rare virtue. After the Fall, sin escalated when

The unacceptable gift

Cain and Abel brought their offerings to the altar. Abel's blood offering of lambs showed a recognition of his need and demonstrated his faith in God, and thus it was received by the Lord. Cain's offering – the fruit of his own labours – was not received. The Lord's rejection of Cain's offering revealed jealousy in his heart, which led him to strike his brother down. When questioned by the Lord, he uttered those shattering words which spoke volumes about the way he viewed Abel: "Am I my brother's keeper?" The answer is that, of course, we are to love and care for one another in the family of God, and that means truthfulness as well as graciousness.

In Matthew 18:15-20, Jesus gives us clear instructions about what to do "if your brother sins against you". Firstly, we are to try to resolve the matter between us; if we succeed at this level, no one else needs to know or be involved. Secondly, if we fail here, we are to take one or two others along. Obviously, they would need to be respected friends who know both parties and are trusted by them. Thirdly, if we are still unable to reach a solution, we must bring the matter to the church. In my understanding that means those Christians who are closest to the two people who are at odds with each other. So this may mean their housegroup or perhaps their local congregation, which would include the leadership, who care for both of those involved in the dispute. We should always keep the circle as small as possible, without wrongly hiding things. In the case of public sin or disagreements which are widely known, there should be some public admonition or statement made. Finally, if anyone is demonstrated to be in sin and refuses to repent and receive correction, they should be put out of the church as lovingly and firmly as possible. Of course, we must bear in

The Forgiveness Equation

mind that the disciplines of the Lord are remedial and intended to bring reconciliation and restoration.

Perhaps for us the nearest thing to "bringing our gifts to the altar" would be presenting ourselves at the fellowship meal or Communion service. Paul warns us of the dangers of eating and drinking unworthily in 1 Corinthians 11:27-32. If there is sin or unforgiveness in our hearts towards other members of the body, we sin against the body and blood of Jesus. The effects of this may be sickness of even death, as we are failing to recognise the wounds we are inflicting on Jesus and on one another. In the light of this, I am amazed at how few churches and fellowships actually practise the simple instructions given by the Lord for maintaining discipline. Perhaps it is because we are in such a weak state of commitment that we have no confidence that they would work. Certainly, when some folk have been disciplined or even simply brought into a confrontational situation, they have walked away in high dudgeon, deeply offended at the thought that there could possibly be anything wrong with them. In most cases they move on to another church, where often they are received without question or reference to the one they came from.

It is difficult to handle a subject such as this in a few paragraphs, but it is such an important one that I did not feel that I could ignore it. I believe that the two main tests as to whether a church is healthy and functional are the presence of both love and discipline. One without the other will mean it is deficient. In order to correct any imbalance it will take more than one person attempting to put things right. There will need to be determined cooperation amongst the leaders and the congregation. But we can begin to prayerfully practise honest and open sharing in our own families and circles of relationships. And where

The unacceptable gift

there is clear immorality of whatever kind, we must bring it to light to be dealt with.

Read: Matthew 5:21-26 & 18:15-20; 1 Corinthians 11:27-32.

Pray: Ask the Holy Spirit for his wisdom to lead our churches into loving discipline. Ask too for a willingness in your own heart to give and receive sensitive correction. Pray for your leaders, that they will not fear confrontation when it is necessary. And pray that this newfound honesty will enable the church to stand against the enemies of righteousness in the world, because they will find no weakness to exploit.

28
Priests forever . . .

You are a chosen people, a royal priesthood, a holy nation, a people belonging to God, that you may declare the praises of him who has called you out of darkness into his wonderful light.

1 Peter 2:9

Once a year the high priest of Old Testament times went into the holy of holies on behalf of the nation to make atonement for their sins. It was a solemn occasion, and God gave Moses strict instructions as to how the ceremony was to be carried out. To deviate from these would have meant death and serious consequences for the people. God, in his holiness, appeared remote and unreachable. The ark of God's presence was separated from view by a veil or curtain of tremendous strength, a constant reminder that even to look upon him would be fatal.

When Jesus was crucified on the cross, at the very moment he died, that curtain was split in two from top to bottom, signifying that the holy place had, at last, been opened up for all men. Now there is a door into the very

Priests forever . . .

throneroom of God, and all who have been sprinkled with the blood of Jesus may enter in. The writer of Hebrews says, "brothers, since we have confidence to enter the Most Holy Place by the blood of Jesus, by a new and living way opened up for us through the curtain, that is, his body . . . let us draw near to God . . ." (10:19-22). When the flesh of Jesus was mutilated and torn apart by sinful men, every cell cried out, "Father forgive them!" And heaven could only respond with a resounding "Yes!" At the same time, that temple veil, which had been the symbol of separation, was ripped in two pieces. Now there is not just one high priest who can come before the Lord on behalf of sinners. There is a whole nation of priests, which includes ordinary, redeemed folk like you and me.

Of course, Jesus will always stand before his Father's throne interceding for us, but today we can join him to pray and seek the Father's face on behalf of others. In the words of Peter, we too have become "a royal priesthood", and our prayers and intercessions can have their effect in the lives of our loved ones, our friends and those for whom the Holy Spirit gives us a burden. Furthermore, we not only have the power to minister to the Lord, but we can also bless and minister the peace and love of God to one another. In the past I have not been a great lover of symbolism. I suppose I grew up as a Christian in reaction to the dead tradition which was crippling the church. People were leaving in droves, tired of liturgies and ceremonies with seemingly little heart or relevance. I still have difficulties justifying much of what takes place in our church worship, but I have begun to see how we can use symbols, beyond bread and wine and the water of baptism, to bless in a very real and positive way.

A few years ago at Spring Harvest, the leadership team felt that after a particular evening message they should provide towels and bowls of water. The dynamics of attempting to

The Forgiveness Equation

organise a full-scale foot-washing in a cold marquee seating thousands of people would have been too much to ask even of such gifted administrators. After prayer, it was felt that people should be encouraged to gather round the leaders of their church or fellowship and simply wash their hands as a way of expressing love and asking forgiveness for not caring more for those who had cared for them. The meeting closed with little groups, some standing, others kneeling, gathered around their leaders, praying and ministering this simple sacrament. There was hardly a dry eye in that huge tent, and many testified to an incredible power and presence of God when they came to physically wash the hands of those who had served them.

I had a similar experience at one of our regular Team Spirit leaders' weekends, which was held at Leicester University. I'd been praying about the closing meeting, where we would break bread together, and had a strong sense that we should also wash the feet of some of the people who were with us. There was a small group of deaf Christians who were working to encourage the integration of the deaf into normal church life. Like many minority groups, they had largely been ignored or rejected by their fellow believers. Then I wanted to pray for one or two young leaders who were with us, as a gesture of our commitment to see thousands of young people released into God's work over the next few years. Similarly I wanted to wash the feet of some of the women, as a sign that we recognised the work God was doing in bringing harmony and a working relationship between the sexes in his church.

All was prepared, but before I could start, Norman Barnes, one of the Team, stepped forward and pulled the rug from under my feet. He proposed that we should start with everyone ministering to Christine and me, and insisted that we sat out front in the very chairs we had provided for

Priests forever . . .

others. Different members of the Team gathered around us and began to wash our feet. The tears flowed as freely as the love and the prophetic pictures of encouragement. What a time of strengthening and healing that was, as that whole group fulfilled a priestly function towards my wife and me. To crown it all, a leader from one of the churches related to us made it practical too by suggesting that, as they were leaving, folk should pop something into our hands or pockets to help with the holiday we were just about to take. As we hugged and made our farewells, notes came at us from all angles as love found a tangible way of expressing itself.

God, being a creative God, will help us find ways of showing our appreciation to those he has given to us and who we count precious. We, being the new and royal priesthood, will find the resources and strength to carry out our role both in the heavenly, spiritual realm and in earthly, practical terms. Our labours should be both hidden and visible, as was the work of Jesus, our great High Priest.

Read: Matthew 27:51-53; Hebrews 10:19-25; 1 Peter 2:4-5, 9-10.

Pray: Call upon the Lord Jesus to pour out a Spirit of intercession on his church, and to raise up men and women who know how to pray as well as how to demonstrate God's love to others. Ask for forgiveness for all the empty words and vain traditions which have not truly represented God's heart. Pray for a wave of creativity which will revive the well-tried means of grace, and will also help us to discover new ways of bringing God's blessing and peace into the troubled lives of so many people, both in the world and in the church.

29
Molehills from mountains

Comfort, comfort my people, says your God . . . her sin has been paid for . . . every valley shall be raised up, every mountain and hill made low . . . And the glory of the Lord will be revealed . . .

Isaiah 40:1-5

What are you, O mighty mountain? Before Zerubbabel you will become level ground.

Zechariah 4:7

"There's no way I can forgive – I'm afraid that nothing will change." "Even if I do forgive, I'll never be able to forget." "The thing I fear most is that if I forgive my feelings of resentment will continue." "Can Satan invalidate my forgiveness by feeding my bitterness?" The last thing our enemy wants is for us to break through into forgiveness, because he knows that it is one of the greatest powers in the universe. Over the centuries he has invented a multitude of devices to keep us from giving and receiving forgiveness. He places obstacles and hindrances in our

Molehills from mountains

path which appear to completely block the way forward. We find ourselves crying out in fear or frustration, "I can't, I can't, I can't forgive!"

Before proceeding, we need to ask ourselves this difficult question: Is "I can't" really a cover for "I won't"? There is a vast difference between the person who has been deceived or deluded by the devil into believing that forgiveness is impossible, and the one who doggedly refuses to forgive. The first is in confusion, while the latter is in rebellion. We have already seen that King Saul refused to avail himself of God's grace. He was cautioned by Samuel, God's prophet, that "rebellion is as the sin of witchcraft" (1 Samuel 15:23, AV). Amazingly, near the end of his life and long after Samuel's warning, Saul was actually found consulting with a witch or medium at Endor.

It is incredible to see how the Lord continued with his efforts to reach the wayward king. In 1 Samuel 16:14 we read that the Lord sent an evil spirit to torment Saul. These words troubled me for ages, until I realised that since Saul had tasted and turned away from God's grace, in his mercy the Lord used evil in an attempt to draw him back to himself. Although Saul did not respond, there are many others who do testify to the fact that after they had disregarded mercy, difficult or even tragic circumstances brought them back to a knowledge of God. The Lord is not unwilling to take serious steps to deter those who tempt providence by walking close to the edge of the precipice. That's the measure of his love; he is not willing that any should perish.

However, for those who are genuinely confused and long for God but can see no way through, there are words of comfort. Hang in there, keep seeking the Lord – the

The Forgiveness Equation

answer will come. God's glory will triumph. Your impassable valley will be raised up, and your unscalable mountain will be made low! God has promised this! Jesus said, "Ask (and keep on asking) and it will be given to you; seek (and keep on seeking) and you will find; knock (and keep on knocking) and the door will be opened to you" (Matthew 7:7-8). He went on to point out that our heavenly Father does not mock us. He does not give us a stone instead of bread or a snake instead of fish; he gives good gifts to those who ask him. We tend to forget that we're in a battle. Satan and his minions struggle to keep us in the dark and apart from God. On the other hand, the Holy Spirit and the heavenly hosts are always striving to break through to us with light and understanding.

Our God is in the business of removing mountains. When we see him, all our troubles, all our questions and all the things which perplex us will come into perspective. But it can only happen when we throw ourselves, with all our doubts and fears, consistently upon him. When a huge mountain stood in the way of the Lord's work in Zechariah's day, the prophet was told in no uncertain terms that the massive obstacle would be flattened, "not by might, nor by power, but by my Spirit, says the Lord Almighty" (Zechariah 4:6). Let me remind you of the story of the unjust judge and the persistent widow. He neither feared God nor cared about men, but she would not be put off. Her constant demands finally prevailed, and he attended to her complaint and saw that justice was done. The parable was not told to demonstrate a reluctance on God's part to listen to those who cry to him, but to show us how much more God desires to hear and answer the persistent prayers of those who seek his face. Rest assured that the Lord does have the answer to your disquiet and concern. In the light of his presence and

Molehills from mountains

wisdom, your mighty mountain will become a mere molehill to be trodden underfoot!

Read: Isaiah 40:1-5; Zechariah 4:1-9; Luke 18:1-8.

Pray: If the Lord has spoken to you about rebellion or witchcraft or indeed any other kind of wilful sin, bring it to him, no matter how much of a battle it is. He will forgive, although that forgiveness may well be contested by Satan. If you have doubts, hold on. Do not let go of God. Thrust your fears, frustrations and concerns, however deep or perplexing, upon the Lord. He is committed to meeting our *need*, even if at this point in time he is unable to answer all your *questions*.

30
Reprise

For if you forgive men when they sin against you, your heavenly Father will also forgive you. But if you do not forgive men their sins, your Father will not forgive your sins.

Matthew 6:14-15

September 15th, 1990 was the culmination of the preparation for the fourth "March For Jesus". During the day I attended our local event and was greatly blessed to discover that there were folk marching in various centres nearby. The final estimate for the British Isles was that around 200,000 people marched in 602 centres – and that does not account for the many "rebel" marches which also took place (about which, incidentally, the organisers were quite happy). In the evening I went along to the prayer gathering at the Westminster Central Hall where Dr Larry Lea from the USA was speaking. My British reserve meant that I needed to be convinced before I gave myself whole-heartedly to the ministry, in spite of all the good things I had heard about the man.

Yes, he was emotional – I can cope with that. Yes, he was dramatic, and used most of the platform to preach –

Reprise

that was okay too. True, he was American and not a little loud – but God loves Americans, so who was I to complain? And . . . the message hit the nail right on the head! Dr Lea is renowned for his teaching on the Lord's prayer, so it was no surprise to me that he used this as his basis for sharing with us. He told us that he had been praying much about what he should say at this particular meeting, where there was such a cross-section of denominations and cultures representing UK Christians. God had spoken very clearly to him about what we needed to hear. He asked us what was the most important section of that prayer which Jesus gave us to pray. I guess we all had our own ideas. "Hallowed be thy name?" "Thy kingdom come?" "Deliver us from evil?" No, the key passage was the one that Jesus re-emphasised at the end of his prayer instructions: "Forgive, so that you may be forgiven."

My heart leaped. I knew that if the church in our nation was going to press through into revival and into all the blessings that God has in store for us, then we must function in forgiveness. Repentance and forgiveness have always been a precursor of revival (or an immediate consequence of it – no one seems quite sure which). We may not be able to make revival happen, but one thing is sure – we can do something about repentance and forgiveness. As Dr Lea went on with his message, he encouraged us to let the offences which come our way move us into a higher place with the Lord. To forgive as we have been forgiven is the key to a release of God's power which would first shake the church and then our nation to the core.

In typical American fashion, with humour and prophetic insight, he exhorted us to deal with our resentments and hurts. "Don't curse it! Don't nurse it! Don't rehearse it! But disperse it and reverse it!" he cried, and I could do nothing but shout "Amen!" at the top of my voice.

The Forgiveness Equation

Cursing, nursing and rehearsing our pains and our problems does nothing to resolve them. Such action may make us feel better for a while, but the difficulties will still be there. Dispersing our troubles by casting them on the Lord will begin a process which ends in a reversal of our circumstances, with good coming out of evil. As I sat listening, I knew that I was to conclude this humble offering of mine on forgiveness by highlighting what Jesus underlined when he taught his disciples to pray. "Forgive us our debts, as we also have forgiven our debtors." Amen!

Read: Matthew 6:5-18.

Pray: Please pray for a mighty breakthrough of repentance and forgiveness in the church. Open yourself up once again to become an agent of God's mercy and grace. Pray that this rising tide of love and forgiveness will overflow the walls of our denominations, churches and fellowships. Then the world will be affected and provoked to acknowledge that Jesus is alive, because they will see him clearly manifested in our love and unity. Cry out to God for nothing less than revival!